Granite
Mtn
THE LIBRARY OF
Hannega
Pea
Creek

OTHER BOOKS BY BEN BEHUNIN

Remembering Isaac
Discovering Isaac
Becoming Isaac
Forget-Me-Notes
Borrowing Fire
Put A Cherry On Top
The Lost Art of Wooing Rabbits and Other Wild Hares
The Disciple of the Wind

Ben's books are available from his website, www.potterboy.com, www.amazon.com and wherever above average books are sold.

A practical FIELD GUIDE

HOW TO SEDUCE A SASQUATCH

THE PRACTICE behind the theory

101 Surefire Ways to Jumpstart Your Creativity

How to Seduce a Sasquatch

First printing, January 2018

Published by
Abendmahl Press
P.O. Box 581083
Salt Lake City, Utah 84158-1083

ISBN 978-0-9998516-8-5

Photography Ben Behunin, Bert Compton
Designed by Ben Behunin and Bert Compton
Layout by Bert Compton

ABENDMAHL
-PRESS-

Dedicated to Ardean Watts
1927-2017
A true Seductioneer

And to my children,
Isaac and Eve.

May your own search for the
Sasquatch prove as joyful as mine.

NOW AVAILABLE IN 3D

FOR THE FIRST TIME!

HOW TO SEDUCE A SASQUATCH

THE PRACTICE behind the theory

SEDUCE

(si-doos, -dyoos), VERB

1. to attract powerfully

SASQUATCH

(sas-kwoch, -kwach), NOUN

1. those doggone creative but sometimes masterfully elusive muses we chase through wood and glen, hoping to catch.
2. another term for Bigfoot

Those who don't believe in magic will NEVER find it.

ROALD DAHL

That truth certainly has implications in all aspects of creativity as well. If we don't believe in creative ideas, it's seems unlikely we will ever discover them. But people are discovering them all the time. Those ideas are out there, somewhere, taunting us to chase them and catch them if we can. Many artists and other creative people I know seem to live their lives in a near-constant state of restlessness, catching whiffs of the magic as it's carried aloft on the gentlest of quiet breezes.

As I have mentioned in some of my other books, seeds for stories and books often blow in on the wind while I'm working in my studio. Some of them land in fertile soil and begin to sprout. Others often sit neglected in dusty corners while I'm working on other projects, and they eventually catch a different wind out of town, where, I can only hope and assume, they are sprouting in someone else's garden.

I may never know what has become of those neglected seeds. And it seems rather counterproductive to focus on the ones that got away. Instead, I have chosen to do what I can to nurture and develop those seeds that put down roots and grow inside my heart and mind.

This is one of those seeds. But unlike many of the more recent seeds that have sprouted in my soul, the germ of this seed has been gestating for more than forty years!

I was just a pup back then–three or four years old–and visiting my grandparents' A-frame cabin in Island Park, Idaho. Many of the details of the trip have faded over the decades, but I do remember the big, yellow moon rising over the ancient pines as we approached the cabin long after dark. I remember the musty smell of that cabin, the snowshoes and rusty bear trap hanging on the wall. But most of all, I remember sitting on an ugly, plaid velour 70s couch and listening to my grandfather tell me the story of the Sasquatch he had tracked through the woods one winter on the very snowshoes that hung on the wall above us.

That night as I sat on the ugly couch, struggling to stay awake as the story was told, I fell under a spell that has never been broken. In the decades that have followed, I have learned that this spell is as old as the world–or at least has been around ever since people have been gathering around campfires to share the legends, myths, and stories that gave meaning and definition to the lives they were living.

On clear nights in remote places where the lights of the city don't spoil the intensity of starlight, we can still experience the magic and wonder of these legends, myths, and stories. In such conditions, magic rises spontaneously like glowing embers on the thermal drafts from our campfires. But those places are becoming increasingly hard to find as cities expand and people conquer the hills and vales and wild places.

And as they do, the bold and mysterious Sasquatches, in all their fabled glory, recede deeper and deeper into the disappearing hinterlands. Yet there are still those who find them. We find evidence of these encounters in the form of blurry photographs and oversize footprints all over the Internet. These sightings leave me encouraged that there are still those who believe in the magic and the legend and are pursuing the Sasquatches if only to catch a glimpse of their unique beauty and mystique.

In every land and continent of the world, we find the oral and sometimes written legends of the elusive, hairy creatures found lurking in quiet, remote places. Some say they are dangerous and should be avoided. Others say they are protectors of the flora and fauna that surround them. Many legends paint them as troublemakers, while others say they are gentle and even kind.

I have often encountered Sasquatches in my travels both near and far. I don't claim to be an authority of any kind but rather a bit of an aficionado.

AFICIONADO

[uh-fish-yuh-nah-doh], NOUN

1. A person who is highly enthusiastic about a subject, activity, or pastime.

(also see enthusiast)

And sometimes I've been called an:

ENTHUSIAST

[en-thoo-zee-ast, -ist], NOUN

1. A person who is highly interested in a particular activity or subject.

There are certainly many who have spent far more

time and effort in both the pursuit of Sasquatches and the study of their habits, environment, and character. I have encountered many of these enthusiasts in my travels. They are often found both at the tops of the mountains and in the deepest of caves. You'll know them when you see them, often curiously sporting both binoculars and magnifying glasses to aid them in their adventures and discoveries. I've found they are generous with both their time and their advice. They are quick to share a story, a smile, and sage encouragement for the journey.

Over the years, I've collected these bits of creative wisdom in my notebooks and sketchbooks. As I've met other Sasquatch Seekers, I've compared these notes with theirs. The bits of creative wisdom I share with you now are by no means complete or comprehensive. They are, however, the best bits of advice I can offer for living a creative life. In the years to come, I hope to be able to share more. Why? Because you've never really lived until you've run with the wind, drunk deeply from the mountain streams, and scaled the gnarliest cliffs in pursuit of the Sasquatch.

Q. BUT WILL I EVER REALLY ENCOUNTER ONE? You might be asking yourself. IS THIS ALL JUST A WASTE OF TIME? A PIPE DREAM? A WILD GOOSE CHASE?

A. That depends entirely on you. You have to decide how far you're willing to go. You have to decide how much time and effort you're willing to dedicate to the pursuit. You have to decide if you're willing to become a full-time Seeker, sacrificing comfort and sleep to photograph and maybe even catch these bold and beautifully elusive creatures. You may find only their markings on trees or their footprints in the deep mud. And you might be content with that. But if you follow these steps and go the distance, I promise your efforts will not go unrewarded.

Q. WHAT KIND OF REWARDS ARE WE TALKING ABOUT HERE? CASH? FAME? LOVE? HAPPINESS?

A. Again, that depends entirely on you. For some, the adventure itself will be well worth the journey. For others, your reward will be found only when you reach the end of the long and dusty road or the top of the distant peaks.

Q. WILL IT REQUIRE A LOT OF WORK?

A. Yes. Absolutely! But it will be the hardest work you will ever love. You'll definitely earn your slumber at the end of the long day. And you better take advantage of whatever sleep you can get, because the rooster will wake you before the dawn and you'll have to go hard again, trying to catch up to a Sasquatch who never sleeps and is perpetually on the move.

Q. SO, WAIT...IT'S GONNA BE TOUGH. IT'S GONNA BE LONG. AND I MAY OR MAY NOT EVER CATCH EVEN AN HONEST GLIMPSE OF A SASQUATCH? WHAT THE HECK?

A. That's right. There is always that risk. But for those who are diligent, open-minded, hard-working, thoughtful, and adventurous, a Sasquatch is never too far away. And once you find one, it's likely you'll find more. In fact, studies have shown that more than 83% of people who have set their eyes on one Sasquatch have gone on to find one or more others. Sometimes they're nearby. Others are many miles and many years apart. But once you've experienced the majesty of a real Sasquatch, you'll never be content with finding a tuft of hair on the thicket or an enormous footprint in the mud. And whether you capture that moment on your camera phone or not, the tales of the journey you'll be able to tell for the rest of your life will certainly make it all worth it.

Q. OKAY, SO IF IT'S REALLY THAT GREAT, HOW AND WHERE DO I GET STARTED?

A. You came to the right place! This is, as far as I can tell, the only book ever written about the lost fine art of seducing a Sasquatch. We, my colleague, Harry von Lederhosen, and I, have included 101 helpful steps to enable you to learn the finer points of Sasquatch seduction. This book of practice, along with the flip-side book of theory, have been designed to increase your prowess, determination, and moxie. The first few may be difficult. Many of them will make you stretch, maybe even think a little differently. But by applying just a few steps to your everyday choices and habits, you'll be on the trail in no time, tracking down your very first Sasquatch. The more steps you put into practice, the more successful you'll be. So hitch up your adventure britches, and strap on your hiking boots. Grab your binoculars, magnifying glass, and butterfly net. Say goodbye to the humdrum forever. From here on out, you're gonna rock this!

PLEASE NOTE: it's not necessary to follow these jumpstart suggestions in any particular order.

#1. BELIEVE

Before you can begin a reasonable search for a Sasquatch, you've gotta believe there's at least one out there; that he can be found, tagged, photographed, adopted, and brought home to camp out in the backyard and that a search for him can inspire you to scale tall mountains and ford bitter-cold streams in his pursuit.

Without this basic belief, searching for a Sasquatch is no more productive than hunting for the Easter Bunny or the Tooth Fairy. You gotta have a real, legitimate reason to embark on this most excellent of adventures–namely, that you're actually expecting to find a Sasquatch. Otherwise, you're only wasting your time and treasure, and you might as well stay home because you're only going to be a wet blanket for rest of the adventurers on the expedition.

#2. BE WILLING TO BREAK THE RULES

I'm not suggesting the need for all-out anarchy. Nor am I suggesting a justification for doping. But many of the things you want are on the other side of the rules that have been holding you back for years. Many of these rules started out with good intentions—namely to keep people from falling off cliffs or wandering into tar pits. But the Seductioneers who enjoy regular interactions with the Sasquatches know that rules have to be bent and sometimes broken. Don't worry, I'm not talking about any moral rules—by all means, hold onto those. But I am suggesting you may be required to trespass, defy gravity, and fight with bare fists and teeth. In the process of breaking a few rules, you will soon recognize that many of the "rules" you've been following all your life are nothing more than recommendations from good-intentioned but often short-sighted individuals and committees who are better suited for government jobs than for creative adventures.

I snuck up on this magnificent creature while he was deeply sleeping.

#3. DREAM BIGGER

Sasquatch seduction is not for the faint of heart, but neither is it for those who don't know how to dream. And we've found a direct correlation between a person's ability to dream above-average dreams and his ability to chase, caress, and commune with the Sasquatches. Nondreamers and small dreamers need not apply. We're talking high stakes here. If you're not there yet, come back when you're ready.

#4. BE WILLING TO CHALLENGE AND CHANGE YOUR THOUGHTS, OPINIONS, AND PREJUDICES

You learn things while you're chasing a Sasquatch that you can't possibly learn any other way. But clinging to old, tired, incorrect, and untrue ideas and principles can and will limit your growth, your ability to understand, and the development of new creative ideas. Don't worry. The things you hold dear, if they are true, will only become more true as you question them, while the things that are untrue will fall away like crusty old barnacles when confronted with freshwater. Like carrying around a ninety-pound backpack, holding onto falsehoods, silly opinions, and prejudices will slow you down, impede your progress, and be a challenge to your floatation as you ford the rivers of adversity. Drop the baggage. A small daypack is all you'll need. Pack only the necessities.

#5. SHED THE FEAR

Though a small level of fear keeps us from making insane choices, fear, in general, is the biggest single inhibitor to all progress, creative or otherwise. What would you be today if you could've made every major decision in the last twenty years without fear? Would you have chosen another path for career, marriage, family, or hobbies? Of their many senses, the Sasquatches have a uniquely strong sense of smell. Studies have shown that they can smell fear from fifty miles away. They are repulsed by it. In a recent interview with a particularly bright Sasquatch, he equated the scent of fear with the vile scent of death. Looking for a fear repellant? Try love. (See tip number 45.)

#6. DARE TO BE YOU-NEEK

Professional People Counters suggest that at least 107 billion people have been born over the history of the world. That's a pretty big number. But the cool thing is that there's only one you in the entire history of the world. And since the beginning, the Sasquatches have always been particularly interested in the people who aren't afraid of being their genuine selves. You don't have to be like everyone else to be beautiful, fun, happy, etc. In fact, to believe you do have to be like everyone else in order to be any of those things is to deny the beauty that is uniquely yours. So stand tall. Let your freak flag fly! Always be yourself… unless of course, you suck. In which case you might consider pretending to be someone kinder, brighter, and happier than you naturally are. (See tip #54)

#7. EMBRACE YOUR INNER CHILD

In order to embrace him or her, you're probably going to have to send out a search party first. And I'm not speaking of the irresponsible, irrational, and immature inner child. I'm talking about the curious, imaginative, and endlessly creative inner child. Most children, when provided with cardboard, twine, sticks, and rocks, can and will create all manner of awesomeness. The Sasquatches are aware of this. They will often put these kinds of materials in your path, hoping that you'll stop and play for a while. When you brush these things aside, the Sasquatches are disappointed. But every time you make the time for creative play, somewhere in the woods a Sasquatch howls with delight. Remember: you were born to create, not just consume. You don't need to spend any money or buy fancy supplies. Remember that children often have more fun with boxes than with the fancy gifts that come in them. You have brains in your head and magic in your hands. You once knew that and didn't even have to think about the act of creation. So let the child out. Make music. Make art. Make happiness. Make believe. Make a difference.

Sasquatch making friends with Bobo The Monkey Girl.

#8. TAKE TIME TO BE STILL

This may sound counterintuitive in our fast-paced world full of deadlines and agendas, but taking the time to sit in quiet places, slow down, and consider bigger things is a silent but strong clarion call to the Sasquatches. Finding stillness can be done wherever you find yourself but is often most effective where you are alone, in a quiet place removed from the chaos of the world. It could be in your car on a relaxing drive. It could be in the bedroom, the bathroom, or the closet. It could be on the top of a mountain or in the middle of a lake on a paddleboard or kayak. It can be done every day. It answers, in part, Socrates's exhortation that "The unexamined life is not worth living." Many of my most profound interactions with the Sasquatches have taken place either during or in direct response to taking the time to be still. Recently I have noticed a resurgence of spiritual practices that employ some aspect of stillness. Whether it be yoga, mindfulness meditation, or just good old-fashioned stillness, the practice offers renewal, understanding, and peace. Who couldn't use more of that?

#9. RECOGNIZE THAT OPPOSITION IS AN ESSENTIAL PART OF EVERY LIFE

Yep, even the mighty Sasquatches have to deal with opposition. Ever flown a kite? Then you know that opposition is required for a kite to rise. And so it is with us. All things have their opposites. Every yin has a yang. Every day has its night. But after winter, there is spring. We can't learn the things we need to learn by avoiding hardship, but I'm also not suggesting we need to seek out difficulty. Hardship, challenges, trials--no one is immune, and no matter how hard we may try to avoid them, they will find us. Be open to them. Be patient with them. Work your way through them knowing they are the string that will allow your kite to not only rise but stay aloft.

#10. FORGET YOUR LIMITATIONS

Whether you feel like your limitations are financial, physical, temporal, or other, you've been putting off your expedition into Sasquatch country for way too long. Studies have shown that when limitations are removed, people are generally more excited about stepping into the happy realm of creative thought and activity. Some of the limitations you have will never go away, while others are chased into the darkness by the mere force of action. So get moving. Do something. Sometimes just a small movement is enough for the clouds of limitation to part long enough for you to see your guiding star. Fences work only for those who can't fly. So wake up. Flap your wings. Rise above the limitations you've been embracing and using as excuses for your inaction. Step out of the fog, and stop the procrastination of your creative future. As you move forward, the Sasquatches will be there to cheer you on as you vault your hurdles.

#11. USE A NOTEBOOK, SKETCHBOOK, OR JOURNAL TO KEEP A RECORD

It doesn't have to be fancy. In fact, fancy sometimes inhibits you from using it. Don't wait for something worthy to record. Put your name on it. Carry it with you always. Open it often. Draw. Doodle. Let your thoughts flow through your fingers and pen. Record the contents of your heart. When used in conjunction with tip #8, this book will be a great tool for recording your progression and your interactions with the Sasquatches.

I love my sketchbooks. I got my first one when I was just eight years old. I've filled at least twenty of them over the years, and I've discovered that the only thing better than a brand-new sketchbook is one that's completely filled. When people say there's no such thing as an original idea, I have to laugh. I have thousands of pages filled with proof to the contrary. A Sasquatch is easily seduced by the blank pages of a notebook or sketchbook. He wants to leave his mark. And for anyone who's listening and anxious to record, he'll sing the creative songs he has to share.

Like I've done with this book, I approach my sketchbooks from both covers. I draw and doodle under one cover then flip the book over and journal under the other cover. When the thoughts and the drawings meet somewhere in the middle, I get a new sketchbook. Besides my wife and kids, these records of my interactions with the Sasquatches are the only things I would run back into my burning house to save. Get one. Use it to make plans, record your thoughts, and dream your dreams. And don't be surprised if you open it from time to time and find the fingerprint of the Sasquatches.

#12. DO YOUR BEST WORK

The Sasquatches I know are never tempted by inferior or shoddy work. They know the difference between someone who is doing their best and someone who's just doing enough to get by. They hate to hear the words, "It's good enough." They know your best work requires more time and effort. And they're willing to wait for it as long as they see genuine intentions. Passion is important to them. They've been disappointed lately that so many people are embracing mediocrity in all its forgettable, uninspired averageness. There is nothing beautiful about mediocrity. If you're going to do anything, make it excellent. Make it the best work you can do. And when you're done, think about how you can make the next project even better. Take notes. Be sensitive and thoughtful. Go at it again with all that you've learned. Excellence requires time and practice, but you'll never reach it or get any help from the Sasquatches if you're not doing your best work every day.

#13. TAKE THE LONG CUT

How we travel is at least as important as reaching the destination. Some people believe getting there is all that really matters. But in the process, they bypass some of the most important stuff. Joyful interactions with fellow travelers, scenic byways, and cozy bed and breakfasts along the way are just a few of the things you'll miss by taking the shortcut. So slow down. The roses along the freeway don't smell anywhere near as bright as those that grow along the country road. And while you're there, don't forget the lilacs and the plumeria. The farmers' stands will have fresh fruits and vine-ripened tomatoes you'll never find at the Quicky Mart along the interstate. And the views from the long cut can't be beat. Pull over and have a picnic, and it's likely a Sasquatch will wander out of the woods and sit down with you on the blanket and tell you stories that will delight even the most impatient traveler.

#14. GET NOT INTO DEBT

The offer of free cash is enticing, but beware– there still ain't no such thing as a free lunch. Beware also that debt is Sasquatch repellent. It squashes dreams and makes slaves of freemen.

My first credit card had a limit of $1500. I knew I didn't ever want to carry a balance and pay interest. I wanted to be earning credit and enjoying the conveniences of having a credit card, but as a young student, I also knew I wasn't even earning $1500 a month. So I called my credit card company and asked for my credit limit to be reduced to $500. I knew I could handle that. There was a long silence on the other end of the line. "Let me get this straight. You want me to reduce your credit limit?"

"Yeah, I want to make sure I don't fall into a hole I can't get out of."

"I've never had any customer ask me to lower their limit. I'll have to ask my manager."

After explaining my reasoning to the manager, my wish was granted. The manager even congratulated me on being a conscientious consumer. It wasn't always the most convenient thing to have a lower limit; it required planning and discipline, but I've never paid a dime in interest. My credit score is awesome. I enjoy the perks of reward miles, and I still pay off my credit cards every month. You can do it too. Challenge yourself to live by the rule, "If I can't pay for it by the end of the month, I don't need it!"

#15. GET OUT OF DEBT

Like fear, the Sasquatches can smell debt from a long way off. It smells like captivity, and in a very real sense, it is. The Sasquatches have difficulty sharing creative ideas with debtors because debtors are constantly focused on the looming rain clouds overhead.

After a divorce, a friend of mine was left with a $20,000 credit card bill his wife had generously gifted him at her parting. He was angry and troubled by the burden. But that week, another credit card offer arrived in the mail offering 0% interest on balance transfers for the first six months. He jumped on the offer and began paying off the interest-free loan. About the time the six months was up, he got a similar offer from another card. He transferred the debt and kept paying. A third interest-free offer allowed him to completely eliminate the debt without paying even a dime in interest. It was a simple, creative solution that saved him thousands of dollars and years of worry. It required discipline and hard work, but after only eighteen months, he was free.

Another friend maxed out a credit card more than a decade ago. She wanted to pay it off but did not exercise the required discipline to eliminate it, paying only the minimum payment (and sometimes late). Last I heard, the original $20,000 debt had risen to over $45,000. She was making decent money and living fairly modestly, but her lack of discipline and the mighty debt were nibbling away at her happiness and freedom twenty-four hours a day. Interest does not sleep. Pay off your debt, or doom yourself to sleepless nights.

#16. STAY OUT OF DEBT

So, once you're out of debt, the next trick is to stay out of debt. Setting up a business can be pricey, and following creative muses is rarely free.

But staying out of debt is not only practical, it's also totally doable.

I built my business slowly, acquiring equipment and materials as I had the cash to do so. With a credit card limit of $500, I had to be creative. I had to save. I had to develop discipline and look for deals and come up with resourceful solutions. I never took out a business loan, and I never had a sugar daddy to help me. It may have been quicker to build my business had I had those things, but having watched my parents lose the family van and a couple of homes due to debt, I knew I wanted to stay as far away from the insatiable monster as possible.

Over the years, I've found that when my needs are greater than my means, a Sasquatch is waiting in the wings, watching my every move. If I yield to the temptation of immediate gratification and pull out my credit card, the Sasquatch turns and runs. But if I choose delayed gratification instead, the Sasquatch becomes my partner, slipping me creative ideas, cheering me on, and pushing me toward alternative solutions that help me maintain my freedom by keeping me out of debt.

When it came time to print my first book, Remembering Isaac, my wife and I had a big choice to make. We had already decided on self-publishing, but as we shopped the book around to local printers, we were shocked by the price tag. Lynnette and I had been saving for several years to add onto our kitchen. Lynnette graciously agreed to postpone that update so we could publish the book without going into debt. Remembering Isaac was not an immediate success (few books are), and I worried for a time that the whole thing might have been a colossal mistake. But slowly, momentum grew. I was able to get the book into a few Costco stores. People started buying it, reading it, and telling their friends. Soon the first printing was gone. We took the money we'd recouped and put it toward the second printing, and then the third. I wrote two more books, rounding out the Niederbipp Trilogy. Each of those printings cost tens of thousands of dollars. It wasn't until three years after we printed the first book that Lynnette was finally able to get her kitchen. But by then, we had decided we shouldn't stop with a kitchen alone. In 2011, we ripped our entire house apart. We added a thousand square feet, gutted another thousand, and put it all back together in a much more functional and creative way. And the best part is that we did it all with cash. No loans. No credit card debt. I'm grateful every day that we listened to the Sasquatches and chose the long cut.

#17. PAY OFF THE HOUSE

At the end of our first year of home ownership, we received a statement from our mortgage company showing us how much we had paid. We'd made twelve payments by then, but this statement showed that the equivalent sum of eleven payments had gone to pay interest on our loan. I was ticked. I did the math. If we waited the full twenty-nine years to pay off our mortgage, we would be paying nearly three times the initial purchase price of the house. I work hard for my money, and I didn't want to see any more of it line the pockets of the banks that really don't care about me.

A Sasquatch heard my frustrations. He gave me some ideas. Over the course of the next six months, I turned my frustrations into a plan. I would pay off my home in twelve years instead of thirty and save all sorts of money. It would require loads of hard work and discipline. Lynnette got on board. We prepared to make some sacrifices. I would give up my Saturdays to attend a farmers market where I could sell my pottery. We would apply the extra $1000 a week from the market directly to the principal on the mortgage. It seemed like a good plan.

I had already found good markets for my pottery. I was sending much of my work to galleries and gift shops on the East Coast. But having a market on Saturdays gave me focus, and my hope that it would pay off my mortgage early made it closer to a laser focus. Each year, we saw the principal declining steadily. It was exciting. If we had extra funds, we would apply them to the principal too. After only six years, we realized we miraculously had enough in our savings to pay off the rest of the mortgage. We did it! And what's even better, we saved over $200,000 in interest. Tax credit, schmax credit.

When we got a financial advisor a year later, he suggested we had cheated ourselves of tax credits and earnable interest by paying off the house instead of investing the money. We may have missed out on opportunities. But we fall asleep every night as soon as our heads hit the pillows, and I never have to worry about losing the house if I have a slow month or quarter. Recently, our financial advisor admitted his envy of a paid-off house.

Work together with your spouse or significant other. Make a big plan. Set some serious financial goals. Keep them. Embrace the wisdom and creative ideas the Sasquatches will whisper in your ears. Reap the unspeakable rewards of financial freedom. If a potter can do it, so can you!

#18. LEARN TO SAVE

When I was a boy of fourteen, my parents fell into financial hardship. They came to me needing to borrow some money. I had saved $3000. They needed it all and more. It would be more than a year before I would get it back. But I was happy to be able to help. (See tip number 19 for the rest of the story.)

Saving is becoming a lost art. Too many people are living paycheck to paycheck. I'm sure this is due in part to people earning just enough to get by. But for most of us in the middle class, not having a healthy savings account is more likely due to our rampant and unfettered consumerism. If we like it, we buy it—right then. We don't wait. We don't save up for it. Fewer people than ever even have a budget. We are largely a nation bent on immediate gratification. And it's killing us. Studies have shown that most people would be in financial trouble if they needed new tires or their washing machine broke. That's no way to live. Surprise repairs and unforeseen crises hit all the time. We need to be ready for them the best we can. Having a nest egg stowed away for a rainy day brings a great degree of peace, freedom, and security.

We have grown too reliant on the safety net. With our nation in record debt, we shouldn't plan on that net catching us. We need to stop acting like irresponsible teenagers and start squirreling away funds for the lean times. You will never regret saving, but you will always have loads of regrets when you need the funds and they're not there. The Sasquatches will help you come up with creative ideas to be able to put away money every month regardless of your income. Learn to live on 80% of your income. Pay your savings account 10%.

Pay God or a charity 10% too. Learning to budget the rest will yield incomparable rewards. And it will slowly starve your self-destructive tendencies toward immediate gratification.

#19. TEACH YOUR CHILDREN TO WORK

The reason I had $3000 when I was fourteen was because I had started working at age ten. My dad couldn't give me much, but he did teach me how to work and provided me with my first lawn mower. I mowed six lawns that first summer. Pushing the mower around the neighborhood, I picked up more jobs each summer until I was mowing forty lawns a week before I left for college. It was good money. It was great training for life, teaching me all sorts of lessons about running a business, budgeting for surprises, dealing with customers, making repairs, saving, and the merits of hard work.

I hired my younger brother to work for me after a couple of years. He took over when I left for school. My youngest brother, Nate, fourteen years my junior, is still mowing some of the lawns I started mowing thirty years ago. Nate worked hard in college; graduated with a degree in business; got a job; and decided after a year that he was happier doing his own thing, working outside, being his own boss. Two years ago, Nate bought the lawn company when my brother Joe left town for a medical residency. Joe had carried the torch for more than a decade, keeping it running all the way through medical school with the help of an employee. He was the only student in his class who was making mortgage payments while going to school. My son, Isaac, age sixteen, has worked for Nate for the past two summers. It's exciting to see the next generation learning these lessons of hard work.

Too many parents are pampering their children today, denying them invaluable lessons that can only hurt them down the road. Do yourself and your children a favor—encourage them to work. Begin when they're small by giving them chores around the house. Any parent who's mowing their own lawn when they have a twelve-year-old in the house is doing that child a great disservice. You may have to put up with crooked lines in the lawn for a couple of years, but crooked lines are well worth the lessons your child will learn in the process. Pull your kids away from the screen and teach them to work, and you'll be teaching them how to fly. Deny them these opportunities, and don't be surprised if they're hanging out in your basement when they're thirty. Man was made to work, and the sooner your children find out there's no such thing as a free lunch, the sooner they'll be able to be independent, contributing members of the world. That and they'll learn for themselves the secrets of seducing a Sasquatch.

#20. PAY YOUR OWN WAY

Remember that no one owes you anything. Don't expect a free ride. Don't expect a free lunch. Don't even expect a discount. Learn to pay not only for your own lunch, but take your turn paying the whole tab. It's good for you. And it's a great way to make friends. The Sasquatches will see your efforts at becoming a contributing grown-up and reward you for your efforts.

#21. COUNT YOUR BLESSINGS

And counting is probably best done, as the hymn suggests, by naming them one by one. When you're feeling blue, count your many blessing. When you've had a good day, count your many blessings. When your dog runs away, count your many blessings. When your car dies, count your many blessings. When you're home sick, count your many blessings. When you're stuck in traffic, turn off the radio and count your many blessings. When you fall off a ladder, get a promotion, get a date, get cancer, kick cancer…well, you know the drill.

Gratitude is the beginning of wisdom. It changes night to day. It helps you see the sunshine even when you're in the darkest of storms. It opens your heart and mind and eyes. And studies have shown that gratitude is like pheromones to the Sasquatches. Open your heart to gratitude, and you'll discover that you're opening your heart to a flood of positivity, creativity, and goodwill. Give it a shot. You've got nothing to lose and a greater understanding of the entire universe to gain.

#22. CHOOSE A DAY ANY DAY (BUT SOMEDAY IS NOT AN OPTION)

Whether you were born a procrastinator or came to it later, you are the only one who can change the direction of your future. You may have bought into any series of excuses. They often come in six-packs, but some people buy the twenty-four-pack—and there are still a few people who buy the whole keg.

If you haven't noticed, the excuses you've allowed yourself to repeat have brought you neither peace nor any closer to achieving your dreams. You can continue to lie to yourself, or you can listen to the gentle whisper of the Sasquatches and decide you're going to make today the best doggone day of your life. And when you wake up in the morning tomorrow, decide to do the same. Better yet, go to bed tonight knowing that tomorrow is going to be the best day of your life. That way you can continue to beat up the inhibitions in your sleep and wake up ready to rock the world with your awesomeness. Someday never has been and never will be a day of the week. Erase it from your vocabulary and get busy.

#23. MAKE YOUR DANG BED

And when you wake up on the best day of your life, you might as well start with making your bed. And why stop there? The Sasquatches love orderliness and cleanliness. They can't think straight in the clutter most of us live with, and they are distracted by chaos. Create a sanctuary where they'll want to hang out. Take out the trash. Throw open the shutters. Let the sunlight in. Crack the window and let in some fresh air. Dust. Organize. Make your space–no matter how humble or opulent–a place where creativity can explode without distractions. You don't need to be a neat freak. But it's important to have a place to sleep and sit and eat without worrying about your health and safety.

#24. ALWAYS HAVE SOMETHING TO LOOK FORWARD TO

Even if it's a full year away, make plans for a trip, an adventure, a rendezvous with a friend. Having something on the horizon helps to keep you focused as you work toward it. It gives you a reason to get up in the morning. It gives you a reason to smile. Without something exciting on the horizon, life is drudgery. And before you come home from whatever it is you've been looking forward to, plan your next adventure. Even if it's just the germ of an adventure, Sasquatches love to see people making exciting plans and will likely throw creative ideas your way to make your next adventure even more exciting.

#25. DROP IT

Whether it's the chip on your shoulder about being cut from the roller derby team or that extra fifteen pounds of baby fat you've been trying to lose since seventh grade, it's time to drop it. You know it's there, gnawing at your soul every day. You may have tried getting rid of it before, but have you ever invoked the power of the Sasquatches for a little help?

Yeah, genetics, bad luck, and bum deals—they're all real, but with the power of the Sasquatches behind you, you'll be singing a new, happier song in no time.

Most of these challenges, and so many more, are due to a very common ailment. Studies have shown that the main culprit is likely a little thing known as confidence. Yep, your confidence tank (CT) may be on the empty side. But lucky for you, a fill-up may be all you need. Confidence can be tweaked, overhauled, and strengthened.

How?

Yep, you guessed it. By embracing the Sasquatches and running the rest of the race with a shot of creativity in your tank, it will feel like you've been taking steroids for years. But the beauty of the influence of the Sasquatches is that there are no negative side effects. With each hurdle you overcome and creative achievement you accomplish, the things that have challenged you for years will begin to slough off and fall away. And in the process, your CT will begin to fill up. Keep it full, and all your dreams will come true.*

*Results may vary, but everyone who embraces a Sasquatch will feel a kick in their pants, a spring in their step, and a zip in their doodah!

#26. QUIT WHINING

Any chump can see the problems, flaws, and failures. They're easier to spot than a Sasquatch at a black-tie dinner. But just seeing the problems and pointing them out rarely does any good. You may have noticed that being pugnacious, confrontational, or bellicose about the problems you notice has done little to help you win friends or influence people in a positive way.

Years ago, I was the president of a co-op gallery at a big shopping mall near my home. With forty-five artists, each with strong personalities and opinions, our suggestion box was always overflowing with mostly negative chatter. Most of it was unusable, angry drivel full of backbiting and name-calling. So we made a change. I informed all the artists that any "suggestion" that was just a whine would be ignored and tossed into the garbage. If, however, they could offer a real suggestion with a prescribed course of action that could plausibly lead to a solution, we would be happy to listen. Things changed. It started slowly, but soon we were receiving all sorts of really creative ideas. We put many of them to work. The feeling among the artists changed from an undercurrent of discontent to real cooperation and friendship. Many of these friendships endure more than a decade after we lost our lease.

I learned all sorts of lessons from the artists in that gallery, but one of the most important is that whining is poison. It hurts everyone who hears it, changes nothing, and produces only more negativity. And perhaps most negative of all, it chases away every Sasquatch for miles around. Upset about something and want to see it change? Invoke the power of the Sasquatches, and allow the creative answers to flow. Stop whining about the problems, and focus your time and efforts on finding a creative solution.

Sasquatch on his first day back to school.

#27. CONSIDER YOUR LEGACY

Over the course of two years, research for my book Borrowing Fire sent me to fifty-eight funerals, fifty-four of which were for strangers. I woke up every morning and scoured the obituaries, looking for interesting people. Then I would go and meet them at their funerals. I wasn't sure what I was looking for at first, but I soon realized I was looking for joy. And I found it. Notebooks full of joy. Over the course of those two years, I wrote several obituaries for myself, considering what I would like to be said in my obituary and at my funeral.

Is it egotistical to worry about what people might think of me after I'm gone? Maybe it is. But I was and am far less concerned about having my horn tooted than I am about making sure I'm doing my part to make the world a little brighter.

What kind of legacy will you leave behind? What will you be remembered for when your actions are weighed on the scales of time? What will the epitaph carved on your headstone say? What will your children, grandchildren, and friends say of you when you are gone? Will they miss you, or will they be singing a rendition of "Ding-Dong! The Witch Is Dead"? How will your life be a blessing to those you'll leave behind?

Think some revisions may be in order? Consult with a Sasquatch. Be open to his creative advice and directions. As C. S. Lewis said, "You can't go back and change the beginning, but you can start where you are and change the ending."

I'm convinced that the world would probably be a kinder, more thoughtful, and gentler place if we each spent a little more time thinking about the legacy we are imprinting on it. Like jet trails across the sky, some fade away quickly, some glow brightly in the sunset, some seem to last forever. Worried about the jet trail you're leaving behind? Consider taking some time to write your own obituary. Date it some decades in the future. Look at it regularly. Revise it as needed. Challenge yourself to be remembered as a jerk by no one.

#28. LOVE GENEROUSLY

Most of us will get only one chance on this planet. Every choice we make creates a ripple effect across time and space. But the ripples that make the biggest difference come from our choices about love.

As it turns out, we have absolutely no control over how people will decide to love us. But we have absolute control over how we love. And how we love affects every relationship we have in life. You can make millions of dollars, plant your flag on the tallest mountains, discover cures for diseases, etc. But if you're a jerk, ain't nobody's gonna miss you.

I've spent a lot of time with older people over the course of my life, and I've learned a lot of lessons from them as they near death. The ones who have learned not only to love but to express their love seem to be genuinely, consistently, and significantly happier than those who have withheld their love or been nonexpressive about it. This and other convincing experiences I'll discuss later have led me to believe that there are two main purposes of life: to learn to love and to learn to eliminate fear. I believe that once we've learned those two lessons, it doesn't much matter when we get called home. So let it out. Let yourself fall in love with everyone you encounter. Love them without judgment. Don't be stingy. Just open up and love! Let it ooze out of you like a gentle river, and your life will be filled with purpose and unquantifiable joy.

#29. GO TO BED

Sounds like silly advice, right? But seriously, sleep is important. It's restorative; healthful; and a required part of every creative, productive life. Whether your body requires eight hours or four, do yourself a favor and go to bed. Staying up to watch TV or play video games is a foolish way to spend your time. An extra hour of sleep can be all that's required for you to have more healthy interactions with the Sasquatches, not to mention every other important relationship in your life. Make it count. Go to bed when you're tired. That sounds so simple, but too many people stay up way past a reasonable bedtime and pay for it the next day. There are plenty of good reasons to stay up late on occasion, but none of us can pull a dozen all-nighters in a row and live to tell about it.

I've found that I can function really well on six hours of sleep a night. Too much sleep makes me tired during the day. Less than six hours, I feel stressed and am vulnerable to sickness. Listen to your body. It's the best tool you have in life. But it won't treat you very well if you don't take care of it. You got a lot to do. Take care of your body, and start tonight by going to bed. Give the Sasquatches a chance to inspire your dreams.

#30. GET OUT OF BED

Studies have shown that the majority of work that gets done in the world is performed by people who get out of bed. Sleeping in occasionally has its merits, but making a habit of it is a colossal waste of time. My most productive hours are from 7:30 to 10:00 a.m. The phone isn't ringing. I'm not interrupted by customers. My head is clear. By the time my teenagers finally get out of bed, I've often put in a half a day of honest labor. Because Sasquatches don't sleep, there are many legends that they are the ones who poke the roosters awake and get the whole day started. If you want a Sasquatch's assistance, meet him as the sun rises and the day is still brand new. You'll be amazed at how much more work you can accomplish just by getting out of bed and getting busy.

#31. MAKE YOUR TIME COUNT

Once you're out of bed, using your time wisely is a huge key in seducing a Sasquatch. As the lucky resident of the First World, life is good for you. There are three square-ish meals a day and clean water flowing from the faucets. Unlike a huge percentage of the world's people, you probably don't have to spend your entire day scraping through the dirt and refuse looking for semi-edible morsels to feed yourself and your children. So what are you going to do with all that extra time?

There's not a lot of fairness in this world. You did nothing to be lucky enough to be born in a country with freedom, internet access, and peace. The folks without those things did nothing to deserve their lot in life either. You don't have to look far to discover huge gaps in equality and fairness. But one thing is equal across all borders: we all have the same amount of time—twenty-four short hours a day.

A friend and mentor of mine used to say, "We're all awake for at least sixteen hours each day. We ought to have something to show for it at the close of the day." When I'm in the studio making pottery, it's easy to look over my work at the end of the day and feel like I've accomplished something. It's a little harder to feel productive when I'm writing, maxing out at about ten pages on my best days. But we are all stewards of time, and I believe there will come a day when we will be held accountable for the time we were given.

How are you making your time count? How are you using it to make the world brighter, better, more hospitable and kind?

Years ago, I recognized that everything changes the hour you realize there are exactly enough minutes for the important things in life. Learn to eliminate the unnecessary expenditures of time, and you will begin to see how truly valuable this finite resource is. As you become more adept at seducing the Sasquatches, you will make every minute count for something awesome!

#32. TURN OFF THE TV

How much of your time is consumed in front of the tube? Studies have shown that the average American over age two spends thirty-eight hours a week watching television! Mind-boggling. And mind-numbing as well. Whether your consumption is above or below average, consider the potential ramifications of walking away from the tube all together.

A decade ago, when I was working on my first book, I was struggling to find time every day to write while trying to keep up with work in my pottery studio. One night, while sitting in front of the TV, I was struck between the eyes by the two-by-four of reality. I never watched a lot of TV—usually just the ten o'clock news and often a Seinfeld rerun afterwards. But I realized that was an hour of quality time without distractions. The kids were in bed. The phone wasn't ringing. My world was quiet and providing me a fine opportunity to write—an opportunity I'd been blowing on stuff that meant nothing. I switched off the TV that night and walked away, never to turn it on again. I'm not sure I've missed anything over the last decade of living a TV-less life, but in that time I've written eight and a half books and read hundreds more, made thousands of pots, spent quality time with family and friends, worked on hobbies, gained valuable education, and occasionally gone to bed early.

In his prophetic dystopian book Fahrenheit 451, Ray Bradbury tells the story of a future world where TV has taken control of society. It's the goal of most people to surround themselves with TV screens, filling each wall of the parlor so they can remain constantly connected with their "friends" in TV land. Firemen are dispatched not to put out fires but to burn books. (The title actually refers to the temperature at which paper catches fire.)

Though we may not have reached the extreme of Bradbury's cautionary tale, we probably aren't too far behind. Every hour we spend in front of the TV is an hour we spend robbing our hobbies, passions, relationships, and innumerable more positive activities. To state it another way, you may not only be neglecting the Sasquatches you hope to seduce, you may also be starving him.

Looking for more time to accomplish the long list of things you haven't been able to get to? I think you just found it. It was there all along—hiding just under the remote's off button.

#33. GET OFF THE COUCH

Okay, now that you turned off the TV, there's not much sense in hanging out on that old, nasty sofa and looking at a blank screen. Get up. Move around. Go outside. Stretch the old (or young) bones. You'll be surprised how just moving your body will inspire all sorts of new ideas that the Sasquatches are anxious to share.

#34. TREAT SOCIAL MEDIA LIKE A TOOL, NOT A THEME PARK

Most of us, if we need a screwdriver, pick it up, use it quickly, and put it away. We certainly don't carry it around all day, fiddling with every screw we come across. Why? Because walking around with a screwdriver in your hand all day is obnoxious, potentially dangerous, and threatening to others, not to mention that it's really difficult to perform your daily tasks if you've always got a screwdriver in your hand.

I'm not going to pretend we don't live in a digital world. It's a reality of life that will never go away and will likely become only more intense. But that doesn't mean it needs to control us. In addition to spending 38 hours a week in front of the TV, the average American spends 4.7 hours a day on their phone! Much of that is spent on social media sites. Advertisers and pornographers alike recognize the power of this trap and use it to exploit us through our digital tethers. We've quickly become a nation and a world of addicts. And though it can be fun and informative, social media, if taken to an extreme—and it very often is—will slowly kill our will to be awesome. We will likely never measure up to the impossible moving target of the alternative reality that is so dishonestly portrayed on these sites. Comparing our lives to those we see on our screens is damaging and demoralizing. Few things cause the Sasquatches to retreat faster into the hinterlands than digital addictions that have stolen our hearts and minds, making us impenetrable to the creative ideas the Sasquatches hope to share with us.

We all know people who have lost their souls, or at least their minds, to social media. I follow my sixteen-year-old son on Instagram and was surprised recently when I noticed he had deleted most of his posts. Why? Because he said they didn't have enough likes! He deleted a record of his life because not enough people thought it was cool!?!

Again, I know social media is here to stay. I have a Facebook page and an Instagram account. I've decided for the time that I will dance with them—but I'm not going to be their date, and I'm staying away from the slow dances. I recognize the power they have to get the word out for my pottery and my books. I like to share uplifting thoughts and ideas. I use them to share pictures of my process and progress. I try to keep it positive and uplifting, but I also post the truth—the reality of my regular failures as well as the tangents and derailments I face as I chase the Sasquatches.

When I think of the trap of social media, I am often reminded of one of my favorite quotes: You may think the grass is greener on the other side of the fence, but if you took the time to water your own grass, yours would be just as green.

#35. LISTEN TO THE RADIO

We all need to be informed, but I've noticed that Sasquatches prefer radio over any other media. Why? Because without visual aids throwing interference, your imagination is constantly at work. I'm not suggesting the same is true with all radio. Commercial radio, with its nonstop advertisements, uber-repetitive songs, and negative talking heads, is probably more akin to a junk food binge than a nutritious feast for the imagination. As a longtime NPR junkie, I recognize the truth of the claim that radio is the most intimate medium of mass communication. Listening to smart, informative, semi-nonbiased radio exercises your creative mind in ways any Sasquatch would cheer. For me, the only thing better than smart radio and informative podcasts is complete silence. Surely there is a time for rocking out to a good 80s pop song, but Sasquatches are sensitive to a lack of moderation. I've found that they will often work subliminally, sending creative inspirations into my head and heart through the stories and discussions found on thoughtful, objective radio programs. Give it a try, and see if you don't feel a little smarter, better informed, and more creative.

#36. TAKE LONG SHOWERS

Okay, so maybe a bath would just work just as well. (I just really hate the idea of stewing in my own juices.) But honestly, some of the world's very best ideas are received in the shower. It makes sense. It's quiet in there. It's warm. You're not distracted by things like phones or kids…or clothes. In such a state, you're vulnerable, and vulnerability is an open door to Sasquatchian ideas.

I usually shower first thing in the morning when the day is new and the thoughts in my head have yet to be distracted by other responsibilities. I often wish I had some waterproof paper and pencils, as many of my more creative ideas come to me as I'm standing under the water–and are too often forgotten by the time I dry off.

Benjamin Franklin was born and lived before the dawn of warm showers, but he recognized the value of daily personal naked time, also known as PNT. Franklin called them "air baths" and suggested naked time was not only healthy for the body but also for the mind.

But if nothing else, a shower is a fine way to get clean. Use a little soap and shampoo, and you're on track for a beautiful day.

#37. BECOME INTERESTING BY BECOMING INTERESTED

Contrary to popular belief, languishing in boredom has never done anyone any good. Studies have shown that boredom causes chronic halitosis; habitual wussitis; and, if left untreated, rump rot. Being interesting may not come naturally to you. It may require constant vigilance to put an end to apathy and indifference. Yes, it might be time to get a hobby, learn to tame lions, take your first jump out of an airplane, enroll in a cooking class, experiment with stained glass, or just go on a walk. Being interesting requires that you to be passionate about something or, even better, many things. Choose at least one. The Sasquatches of creativity will honor you for it and bear you gifts of happiness and friends. No one likes a bore.

#38. GO SKINNY DIPPING

The idea for this one came from a photography workshop I attended last year. The instructor shared with us the advice he'd been given by his professor years before when he asked for advice about taking more interesting photos. The professor's advice was simple—only three words: go skinny dipping.

It made me laugh when I first heard it, but I realized there's a lot of wisdom packed into those three words. If you're a regular skinny dipper, chances are you're living a rather interesting life. You're not being held back by norms, social expectations, or small thinking. You're going to be adventurous, easygoing, and fun loving. And it will put you in a place of regular if not perpetual vulnerability. (See tip #40.)

As an opportunistic skinny dipper myself, I've learned there are things you can experience in your birthday suit that you can't learn any other way. But many of these things can also be learned as we allow ourselves to let go of our inhibitions, embrace our vulnerabilities, and become less afraid to resist the pressure to cave to social norms. As we allow ourselves to run wild and free—either figuratively or literally—our actions will go far to seduce the Sasquatches.

#39. GET YOURSELF A MENTOR

No matter how smart, charming, talented, or creative you are, there is always someone smarter, charminger, talenteder and creativer. And thank goodness there is, because evolution is an essential part of staying vibrant and alive. Find one of those people who are more somethinger than you are. Strike up a conversation. Take them to lunch. Pick their brain. Convince them to let you tag along on an adventure.

I've made a habit of always having at least one mentor. Recently I lost one of my favorites, Ardean Watts. Ardean inspired me by rebelling against all that is normal, commonplace, and small-minded. He was a born adventurer, a musician, a rabble-rouser, and probably the most passionate person I've ever known. He had a huge library filled with books on every subject. He'd read them all multiple times. He had years of stories on the tip of this tongue and was always willing, even anxious, to share.

Ardean and I shared an interest in wild mushrooms. He had become such an expert that Poison Control called him every time they got a call about a potential poisoning. He would drop by my studio from time to time with fire in his eyes, telling me the conditions were right to hunt for mushrooms. We'd drive together to secret places near and far, where we'd find all sorts of awesome mushrooms. If I were out fishing or hiking and stumbled upon mushrooms I wasn't familiar with, I'd take them to him to identify and teach me. He was always anxious to impart his knowledge and wisdom.

Ardean passed away in 2017. I've missed our visits and chats. He inspired me to stretch, to think harder, to open my heart and mind and eyes, to be perpetually and passionately curious. He, more than most, knew and comprehended the clarion call of the Sasquatches.

Mentors can come in all ages, genders, nationalities, persuasions, and interests. It may be possible to seduce a Sasquatch without one, but a good, strong, creative mentor can make the journey exponentially more enjoyable. I suggest finding a good one. And when he or she dies, find another. And when the time comes that your wisdom and experience allow you to be a mentor yourself, be as generous as possible as you share with your mentee the joyful song of the Sasquatches.

#40. ALLOW YOURSELF TO BE VULNERABLE

It's in our best interest to protect ourselves. We are naturally inclined to seek out comfortable places away from the cold, harsh realities of life. That natural inclination has kept us alive, out of danger, and away from troubles. It's part of who we are as homo sapiens. And we should all be grateful for those natural, inbred propensities. But the gift that previous generations have given us can also lead to our stagnation and even our downfall. Comfort can and will retard our growth.

Allowing ourselves to be wisely and selectively vulnerable is an essential ingredient to personal growth and every interpersonal relationship. It requires that we lay down our arms for a time and be open to new experiences, insights, and feelings. Not allowing ourselves to be vulnerable will slow if not entirely halt our learning and progression. Voluntarily embracing the notion of vulnerability throws open the door to experiences of all kinds. It requires wisdom and understanding to decide what to allow through that door and what to turn away. But by keeping the door as open as possible, we will be provided with experiences and knowledge that will bless our lives in ways we never could have imagined if we had kept the door closed.

Living their lives without either clothing or what we would consider adequate shelter has taught the Sasquatches great wisdom. Learning to discern the Sasquatches' voices and meaning will help you to know what can reasonably be invited in and what should be turned away at the door.

#41. TAKE TIME TO PLAY

As any experienced Seductioneer will tell you, the Sasquatches are a playful bunch. And by taking the time to play, you will be inviting the Sasquatches into your life. For many of you, it's probably been a long, long time since you took the time to play. Studies have shown that adults who stop playing turn into utter bores. If left untreated, they can dissolve into gigantic black holes, sucking up all the joy around them.

Studies have also shown that children learn more from play than they do from nearly any other experience or activity. Imaginations are developed. Creativity blossoms. Ideas grow and mature and turn into all manner of awesomeness. It's messy and fun and amazingly beautiful.

So why do we stop building blanket forts and climbing trees and making mud pies? If these activities brought us so much joy, why did we ever stop? The joy we experienced in those raw, unfiltered, organic activities helped to make us who we are. After spending our first five years running wild and free, we spent the next thirteen years having the wild drilled out of us. Is it any wonder why we turned out to be boring adults?

Einstein was once asked, "If you could attribute your success to one thing, what would it be?" His answer is telling: "I never lost the ability to think like a child."

That's not an easy thing to do, especially with our education system, tiger moms, and helicopter parents trying to beat the wilds out of us and turn us into respectable people. But can't we have it both ways? Can't we be respectable while nurturing the playful child within us? Einstein seems to suggest that not only is it possible, it could also be incredibly useful.

So pull out the Play-Doh and rig up the blanket tents tonight. Your kids and grandkids will love you for it, and you'll unlock the door to that dreadful cell where your inner child has been wasting away for decades. It will only take the scent of bottle rockets and a little good old-fashioned dirt under your fingernails to revive him or her. You'll be climbing trees and running around in airplane formation in no time.

Whenever my work begins to feel a little stale, I recognize that though I play around in the mud all day every day, my work can still become rote and unnaturally mechanical. It takes practice to break through that, but unfettered play is always the antidote.

Children know the song of the Sasquatches by heart. Even though we have to grow up, that don't mean we have to grow old. And no matter how long we've ignored it, the song of the Sasquatches still bounces around in the secret chambers of our hearts. Learn to play again, and let it out.

#42. CREATE AND MAINTAIN A CURIOSITY LIST

Call it what you will, but having a list of things that make you curious is a great way to keep you ever learning. Always wondered why and how the moon affects the waves of the sea? Wondering how to regrow hair like Donald Trump? Put it on the list.

And then when you have an evening with no plans, get out your list. Educate yourself. Do a little research. Most of us have the Internet in our homes and therefore have more knowledge and up-to-date information at our fingertips than could be stored in a thousand libraries.

The Internet can be a black hole that has the potential of sucking you in and spitting you out on an inhospitable, distant planet. But it can also be an amazing tool for accessing awesomeness. Creating a curiosity list will also summon the interest of the Sasquatches, allowing you to make the best use of your time while helping you to maintain your interest and focus.

#43. NO PATH, NO PROBLEM

The lonely truth is that if you're on the path of discovery, it's likely there won't be a path at all.

Many times in the last twenty-two years, feeling disoriented and confused, I've wondered where I'm going and what I'm doing. That's rarely a fun place to be. Okay, sometimes it really sucks. Limbo, after all, feels worse than hell. At times like this, I've relied heavily on my faith, spent a lot of time talking to my wife and my mentors, and wandered off to the woods to consult the wisdom of the Sasquatches. Answers come. New directions appear. Vision, at least for the next step or two, opens to my view. I have often thought that if I knew another potter/writer he might be able to point me in the right direction. But I don't know anyone who has trod this same path before. And that's probably a good thing. I am on a path of discovery. It's rocky. It's steep. And all uphill. And as luck would have it, there's no trail as far as the eye can see. I've had to trust my faith and the distant call of the Sasquatches to guide my feet. It's worked out so far.

Don't be afraid to wander off the well-worn path. It's where all the magic I've ever experienced has taken place.

#44. GET YOUR BUTT OUTSIDE

Nature is one of the greatest teachers. Inspiration is available with every step and under every rock. Take time to examine the miraculous and beautiful minutia. My work is constantly being influenced by my regular jaunts out-of-doors. The song of the Sasquatches is filled with verses about the flowers and the trees, the rocks and the grasses, the rivers and the sea. Go outside. If you're listening, you'll hear it too.

#45. MAKE YOUR OWN LUCK

We've all seen people at the top of their game and marveled how lucky they are to be there. I've discovered that even though luck often plays a role, luck rarely happens on its own. The award-winning Polish-American filmmaker Samuel Goldwyn said, "The harder I work, the luckier I get."

There's a great truth in that. I've met many millionaires in my lifetime and had a chance to talk with many of them. Their sentiments about their rise to the top of the food chain have all jibed with Mr. Goldwyn's. It's far less likely that you'll ever win the lottery than it is for luck to be on your side if you simply get to work.

And Seductioneers all agree—the luck of the Sasquatch follows those who pull their hands out of their pockets, put on their work gloves, and work their butts off.

#46. CREATE A POSITIVE ZONE

It's hard to create anything beautiful if you've got someone nagging at you all the time. This is especially true if that voice is coming from inside you. You don't need that. And it's unlikely you'll be able to move forward if you're constantly bombarded by negativity.

What you need is an antigravity chamber. But since we're not really sure if they exist, and since they'd probably be cost prohibitive if they did, we need a better solution. A roll of brightly colored masking tape will do the trick. Lay it down across the threshold of your creative space. Maybe wrap it around the whole doorway. Let your friends and family know that when you're in your positive zone, you'll have no patience for negativity. Then tell yourself the same thing. You might have noticed that positive and possibility share the same prefix—pos, which, if I remember my Latin correctly, means "of or relating to awesomeness!" Who doesn't need a whole lot of that in their lives? We all need a safe space where magic doesn't have to compete with the negative voices of Muggles.

#47. GO STACK SOME ROCKS

For millennia, people have marked their paths with cairns--a fancy name for piles of rocks. On every continent, cairns can be found, offering hope to weary travelers, assurance that they're still on the right path.

In Sasquatch lore, cairns were originally the work of the Sasquatches, built to lure the more adventurous travelers onto more exciting paths.

As you forge your own long and dusty road, take a minute to stack up a couple of rocks when you stop for water or to set up camp for the night. Leave a sign that someone else made it this far. It may be years before someone trudges over the same tundra, but they will see your cairn and be heartened by the fact that they're not alone in their quest. They may follow your path for a while before branching off on their own.

The road of creativity is filled with many challenges. Do not try to remove them. They are there to strengthen those who choose the long run—the road less traveled. But a friendly cairn along the way always goes a long way to encourage fellow travelers to carry on in their own adventures.

#48. PLAY TO YOUR STRENGTHS

It's never impossible for a three-foot-tall, one-armed man to become a lumberjack. All of us are capable of rising to meet great challenges. But each of us has been blessed with natural strengths and abilities. If you don't know what yours are, ask your friends and loved ones to point them out to you. There will be plenty of time to work on overcoming weaknesses and deficiencies. But let's work on honing your strengths first. Great confidence comes from exercising and developing our God-given talents. And great confidence will be necessary as you work to overcome your weaknesses. Life, for most of us, spans many decades. If you pace yourself and keep working hard, there will be time for everything that's important. And at every challenge you endeavor to conquer, the mighty Sasquatches will be nearby, cheering you on.

#49. RECOGNIZE THAT YOURE IN GOOD COMPANY

The first five words of the Bible are encouraging for any creative soul looking for adventure:

In the beginning God created…

How cool is that? And if you believe like I do that we are the spiritual children of God, we would naturally have to believe that some of His creative attributes and genius have rubbed off on each of us. I guess that makes us junior creators. We may not have the same omnipotent power as our Heavenly Father, but we've still got some powerful juice in us!

And looking a little closer down to earth, humanity has been driven to create long before we could read or write or even converse with our neighbors. It's in there—somewhere—in each of us. A drive for self-expression. Dwellers of the caves felt a drive to brag about the animals they were barbecuing. Others boasted about the grain they were growing. Clay workers created functional pottery and religious effigies. Basket makers and weavers created beautiful things to use every day. The need to create dwells in each of us in one form or another and screams to get out. If we suppress it, we deny part of that which is holy within us. If we let it out and work to polish our skills and talents, we'll not only have the approval of the Gods, we'll also have the encouragement of the Sasquatches.

#50. PACK YOUR OWN PARACHUTE

Ain't nobody ever gonna care if you live or die more than you do. Don't put your future in anyone else's hands. As you take responsibility for yourself and your choices, the Sasquatches will back you up and cheer you on to victory. If you make a bad choice, own it. Learn from it. Move past it. Never blame anyone for your choices or failures. Never accept all the credit for your triumphs.

#51. NEVER SET UP CAMP IN A SWAMP

Winston Churchill wisely admonished, "If you're going through hell, keep going." We all have to pass through hard times, but the secret is to pass through them and not take up residency. There are better days ahead, but only if we trudge through the mire and head for higher ground. It will get better. It always does. So lift up your head. Orient yourself with whatever sun you can find poking through the clouds, and head out in the direction your heart tells you is right. The Sasquatches will see your efforts and set up cairns along your way.

#52. DO YOUR OWN STUNTS

Few names elicited the same level of awe and acclaim among my young peers as Evel Knievel, the courageous daredevil in yellow leather. He was all the rage back in the 70s, jumping his motorcycle over cars, cement trucks, and even the Grand Canyon. We'd often attempt to copy him on our BMX bikes. It would be a success no matter what, as long as we didn't end up goosing ourselves on the crossbar or handlebars.

The coolest thing about Evel was that he was an inspiration for a whole generation of boys, and maybe their dads too. He inspired us to overcome the difficult and attempt the impossible. He taught me that with the right planning and preparations, no stunt was too big. Nothing was out of reach.

Many of the stunts you'll attempt will look impossible. You'll hear from plenty of doubters and naysayers. Some of your stunts will flop. You may break a few ribs and spend some time in the hospital. But the downtime will give you a chance to rethink the challenge. The Sasquatches will inspire you with all sorts of solutions you never considered. And when you finally fly over your own Grand Canyon, you'll be praised for your bravery and called a hero. The world needs more people who specialize in the impossible. You might as well be one of them.

#53. DONT STOP AT THE HORIZON

For centuries, if not millennia, it was a common belief that the earth was flat and that one could literally sail off the edge of the earth and be lost forever. And though few people still believe the earth is flat, plenty of people allow fear to keep them in safe, comfortable places where they might never come close to falling off the edge of the earth.

You can't hang out with people like that and not be affected by their small minds and pathetic warnings of doom. Find a group of fellow explorers who will encourage you to go further than you've ever gone before. If you never push the limits, you'll never find out that the only real limits are the ones you believe in.

My father told me repeatedly that I would never be able to support a family with pottery. Why? Because he'd never known anyone who had. He told me the same thing when I started writing. I listened and didn't write for a year and a half. But fortunately the Sasquatches were louder, repeatedly telling me that I had to try. If I'd believed my dad, I would have missed out on a really fulfilling life.

Successful explorers don't stop at the horizon. They don't believe the bellyachers and party poopers. They push on. And when they reach the horizon, they wave goodbye to the naysayers back home and keep going, further than anyone has gone before.

#54. FULFILL THE MEASURE OF YOUR CREATION

It will likely take the full extent of your life to discover, work toward, and ultimately realize the purpose of your life. Many people catch glimpses of their divine purpose, but after realizing how much work it will take to achieve it, they put things on hold and never get back to it. I'm not sure if it's possible to reach fulfillment without a relationship and partnership with God. After all, He created you. He knows your talents and value. You will need His help to overcome the challenges ahead. There will always be opposition to your efforts as you work to fulfill the measure of your creation. But God will awaken your strength to overcome all of your challenges as you rely on Him and consult with Him frequently. I have learned that the full measure of our creation will always be exponentially bigger than we imagined it would be and it may take us in very different directions than we ever would have guessed. But if we allow God to shape us and prove us, we'll discover His plans for us are infinitely better than anything we could have come up with on our own.

#55. INCLUDE GOD

By cutting the Creator of the universe out of our lives, we limit our future to the borders of our own imagination. And even if those borders are big and ever expanding, we'll forever be pipsqueaks compared to the God of heaven and earth. I believe He is anxious to help, encourage, and inspire us. But He will never force Himself upon us. He waits patiently to be invited in. And when we do, there ain't no mountain we can't climb with His help.

#56. PAY A TITHE

Since the beginning of recorded time, humanity has been commanded by God to pay a tenth of our increase as a tithe. Through the prophet Malachi, God promised all mankind that if we put Him to the test and do what He asks us to do, He will open the windows of heaven and pour out His blessings upon us to the extent that we won't have enough room to receive it.

From my youth, I have kept the law of the tithe. And I have continually experienced the promised blessings. The Sasquatches have inspired some pretty cool things, but every truly great thing that has happened to me, my family, and my business, I attribute to God and the blessings of living this law.

On one hand, 10% is a big pay cut. On the other hand, everything I have and am has come as a gift from God. Compared to the government, God really doesn't ask much in return. And I've learned that no matter how much I give to God, he returns it all to me—and so much more. No matter what we give back to God, none of us will ever be able to be square with Him. Put God's promises to the test in your own life. If it works out, great! If it doesn't, well, it's still really good karma. I have faith enough to say it will work out and it will change your life forever in the process.

#57. NEGLECT NOT THE GIFT THAT IS IN THEE

God plants in the heart of every human being a seed of light and talent. When we exercise and

develop a talent, the light attached to it burns even brighter, illuminating our world. We must make the decisions about how we will use these amazing gifts. If we neglect them, the light is diminished and the world is cheated of the potential light. Decide to let your light shine by nourishing your beautiful and unique gifts. Keep your talents exercised, and they will bless you and all who know you.

#58. BE SOBER

It's a common cliché that creative people often fall into the deep, dark trap of addictions. Perhaps it's self-medicating for pain. Perhaps it's out of boredom. Perhaps we're looking for inspiration. Whatever the case may be, addictions of any kind will only hurt you and sap the light away from your creative spark and gifts. The Sasquatches hate being around drunkards and have no patience with the stoned.

I made my decision to never drink when I was twelve years old. We were visiting my grandfather at a veteran's hospital, where he'd been convalescing for several months after a stroke. My grandfather was a creative man and a hobby sculptor, but all of that ended with his stroke. A company buy-out twenty years earlier had forced him into retirement at age fifty-five. In his boredom, he backslid into some habits he'd acquired in his youth and during the war. He smoked and drank for many years, refusing his doctor's orders to quit. The stroke left him paralyzed and unable to communicate. He languished in a vegetative state for five long years before he passed away, leaving my grandmother alone until her death twenty years later.

None of us have to look very far to find addicts in our family tree. It's in our blood. We are free to choose captivity or freedom. But know that the Sasquatches of creativity always prefers freedom and is repelled by the stench and rot of captivity. Choose sobriety. Choose freedom. Drugs are a broken, unreliable crutch—lean on that crutch, and you are doomed to fall.

#59. PLAN FOR THE FUTURE

Working with clay has taught me the importance of planning for the future. Most of my projects require about two weeks from start to finish. There's making time, drying time, firing time, glazing time, and firing time again all require patience and planning.

Similar steps and timing are required in our lives in order to avoid too many stresses attacking us at once. It will always be true that the best time to plant a tree is twenty years ago. But the second best time is today. It's as difficult to build a tree fort in a sapling as it is to begin at age sixty-four to plan for retirement. There will always be surprises. As the Yiddish proverb goes, "Man plans and God laughs." But working toward a goal, even if it's a moving target, is better than ignoring and neglecting it all together. Save for the rainy day you know will come. The Sasquatches always suggest keeping one eye on the road immediately in front of you and one eye on the horizon.

#60. LIVE IN THE PRESENT

The past has come and gone. There's nothing you can do to change it. The future has yet to be written, and there's much we can do today to influence it. But there's no time like the present. It's really the only time we have much control over.

I mentioned my friend Ardean Watts in tip #39. Ardean and his wife, Elna, were married more than sixty-five years before he passed. I asked them on one occasion if they had any secrets for a long and successful marriage. Elna's answer was quick:

"We decided when we first got married that we'd never quarrel about anything that was more than two weeks old." I know my parents' marriage could have been saved by adopting this sage advice, and mine has been strengthened by it too.

When we live in the present, the Sasquatches of creativity are able to employ their full arsenal of tools. Each day is a new day. Like a field of deep, fresh, unmarked snow, it is full of potential and endless possibilities. Make it count for something awesome by focusing your attention on it alone. Tomorrow you will have a new day, a new fresh field of snow. What you learn—or don't learn—today will likely influence what you learn—or don't—tomorrow. Make today count. Make every day count.

#61. BE PRESENT

Showing up to work is an essential part of keeping a job. Showing up to your wedding is an essential part of being married. Being late for either one will likely result in some negativity. Showing up to either one physically but not mentally, emotionally, or spiritually isn't much better than not showing up at all.

Being present requires that we focus our five senses on what's within ten feet of us. Thousands of accidents occur every day because people allow one or more of their senses to become distracted. Living in the digital world with all of its bells, whistles, and disturbances requires self-control, vigilance, temperance, and discipline. I'm convinced that most of us miss the Sasquatches that are dancing all around us every day because we're distracted by far lesser things.

#62. DO MORE STUFF THAT MAKES YOU FORGET YOUR PHONE

There are certainly unlimited reasons for you to be constantly picking up your phone, but let's face it—your addiction has become a mammoth distraction. The average American checks her social media sites fourteen times a day. In Asia, it's closer to forty! The time we spend on our phones (4.7 hours/day!) is valuable time. If you could redirect even half of it to fulfilling the measure of your creation, just imagine how awesome you could be. Instead of reaching for your phone when you're bored or have a minute of downtime, reach for your sketchbook, your didgeridoo, your ukulele, your knitting, your lover, etc.

You admire the talents of others and wish you had some of your own, but you just can't find the time to work on anything? If you're an average American, you now know where you can find at least

4.7 hours a day. Man, that's a lot of time! Plenty of time to write a poem, read several chapters in a book (or maybe write a few pages of your own), practice an instrument, paint a picture, or have a great visit with a friend. Remember: Everything changes the hour you realize there are exactly enough minutes for the important things in life. Stop trading your diamonds for common stones. Set a goal to not pick up your phone—except maybe to talk to someone—until you've spent at least an hour each day working on your own brand of awesomeness. The Sasquatches will inspire your efforts if you're open to creative suggestions.

Camping with the homies

#63. TAKE A VACATION

The Sasquatches are waiting to surprise you, but you gotta step away from the distractions of work, home, and responsibilities. A vacation doesn't have to be expensive; in fact, my family's favorite ones have cost very little. Not having funds for elaborate getaways can actually be a creative blessing. If you're looking for a truly creatively rejuvenating experience, pack a few basics, flip a coin, and head out for Sasquatch country. Don't make any plans. Try to get lost by taking every detour, side road, or diversion you can find. Focus on the journey rather than any destination. Sleep under the stars. Get up in time to watch the sunrise. Try out the mom-and-pop diners you discover along the way. Stop and ask locals for suggestions.

One of the great perks of being self-employed is the ability to take as many vacations as I want. Sure, I may not make any money while I'm gone, but the trade-off of filling my brain with new images and experiences is better than any amount of money I could earn if I stayed home. My wife and I didn't have much money when we got started. Our first trip as a married couple was two weeks of camping on the Pacific Coast Highway from Seattle to Laguna Beach. We spent $600, made amazing memories, and filled our canteens with some of the most delicious creative nectar we've ever tasted.

I love the way I feel when I'm in a place I've never been before. My curiosity is on overdrive, my eyes are wide open, and I overflow with adventurous energy.

Get out of Dodge. Raise the sails of adventure. Get lost. And don't come back until you've filled your canteen.

#64. TAKE REGULAR VIRTUAL VACATIONS

What, no time to get away? Or maybe you just got back and have to wait for your vacation days to accrue again? No problem. With the click of a mouse, a little time, and the spirit of adventure, you can take virtual vacations every evening. Granted, they're pale shadows of real vacations, but they can fill your head with some semblance of the images and experiences of actually being there and nurse the thirst for adventure. Take your spouse and family along with you. Let them drive the mouse for a while. Teach them that the world is round and beautiful and breathtakingly amazing and diverse.

With an open mind, the Sasquatches of adventure can inspire the whole family to think bigger, bolder, more colorful thoughts.

#65. BRANDISH THE POWER OF LOVE

There are many motivators in life. Fear. Money. Power. Fame. But the most powerful is and always will be love. Loving your job will make it easier to do and allow you to spread some sunshine along the way. There is nothing in this world that Sasquatches are more attracted to than love. Their excitement when they feel it causes them to erupt with exuberance. I suppose that shouldn't surprise anyone-we, after all, do the same thing.

If your main motivator in life is something other than love, perhaps it's time to examine your life and make some changes. Love doesn't only make the world go round better than anything else-it also makes life worth living. If you can find a way to inject love into everything you say, think, and do, your life will be filled with friends, success, and meaning. Every other motivator falls flat and pales in comparison to the great, endlessly enriching, and intoxicatingly wonderful power of love.

#66. HAVE FUN

Similar to the power of play, the power of fun is not only essential in the art and practice of successful Sasquatch seduction, it is also a vital ingredient of a happy life. Most people don't know it, but fun is actually a muscle that must be exercised. Left dormant, it will shrivel and atrophy and induce chronic constipation. If this condition is left untreated, it will cause its sufferers to turn into feeble, little-minded prunes. And ain't nobody got time for prunes.

Exercising your fun muscle may take some practice if you're a little rusty. But you will soon discover how much more attractive you've become, not just to the people around you but also to the Sasquatches. Allow yourself to have fun. Learn to laugh at yourself. Make jokes, especially those that are self-deprecating. Be generous with your smiles. When you're tempted to be a prune, stop and have fun instead.

#67. BE FUN

Having fun is one thing. Being fun is several steps above. It's certainly within reach of everyone, but it requires consistent and regular flexing of the fun muscle. I've discovered that those who've learned to be fun usually have a whole herd of Sasquatches camping in their backyard, popping corn and swapping tales.

Since my childhood, I've always admired adults who were somehow able to hang onto a fun-loving nature and keep their fun-fitness robust and healthy. My own father lost his sense of fun early on. One night when I was in high school, I was visiting a good friend and her parents, enjoying laughter and good times in their kitchen. I realized it was the first time I'd had fun with adults in a long time. Before I left, my friend's father, a professional ophthalmologist, wrote my father a prescription—for an enema! My father didn't think it was very funny. Prunes don't like to look in the mirror. Whenever I find myself getting uptight with my own teenagers, I remember that prescription. Nobody likes a grumpy prune, but all the world loves to be around someone who's fun.

#68. WEAR FUN

The clothes we choose to adorn ourselves with say a lot about us. Wear a three-piece suit with a starched shirt and a black tie to an informal party or concert, and you're probably not going to make many new friends.

When I was in high school, I started rebelling against the social norms of fashion and began donning a bow tie for events where a tie of some sort was appropriate. It felt good to be able to express my rebellion in a harmless way. I carried that tradition with me to college and onto my LDS mission in Europe. I'd get a lot of double takes. I could see the cogs in people's heads turning as they looked at me, and I could almost hear them thinking, "This kid's either a nutcake or an eccentric, but either way, he's different. I want to know what's inside that goofy head of his."

But beyond the reactions I'd get from others, I recognized that wearing a bow tie somehow empowered me with a genuine superhuman ability to be friendly. You just can't wear a bow tie and cranky pants at the same time. I discovered that there seems to be an unwritten law in the universe that if you wear a bow tie, you have to smile—there has to be a streak of fire…or at least a vein of goofiness… somewhere in your soul. I've found that most people are attracted to goofiness like they are to fun.

To this day, I wear only bow ties when a tie is called for. But I've also added some other accessories that make my children blush. I found a killer pair of bell-bottom, plaid golf pants at a thrift store a decade ago. I call them my Party Pants. My sister-in-law still tells me that whenever she's feeling blue, all she has to do is remember me in my plaid pants and bow tie, ripping it up on the dance floor on a cruise we all went on ten years ago.

My children have been especially been mortified by several pairs of shoes I've acquired over the last few years from a cobbler artist. They're kind of a mix between clown shoes and bowling shoes—mismatched, bright colors; painted scenes like cacti and octopi on the toes; and florescent laces. They make me happy, start plenty of conversations, and make people smile.

Clothes say a lot about us. The Goths know this. Their clothes scream, "Don't talk to me. I'm angry at the world. I don't have time for you. I may be dangerous." It may not be fair, but people are always making judgments about what we wear and how we wear it. I've decided to confuse them, to keep them guessing, and to try to be as friendly and as open as possible. Give it a try. The Sasquatches will applaud you.

#69. BANISH MEDIOCRITY

Brian Wilson wisely warned, "Beware the lollipop of mediocrity; lick it once and you'll suck forever." It feels tragic to see mediocrity taking the place of excellence in every aspect of our lives from our interpersonal communication to the work we produce. I swear, if I hear my kids say, "It's good enough," one more time, I'm gonna scream. The it's-good-enough mentality has infiltrated our world, dropping its insidious hooks into everything. Shoddy, inferior craftsmanship is swamping our stores, our homes, our televisions, and our very lives. Only you can stop mediocrity. Refuse to buy it. Refuse to make it. Refuse to accept it. Demand excellence instead. Go the extra mile. Do your best work. Put some heart into it. The world, as well the Sasquatches, will reward you handsomely for it.

#70. GO OFTEN TO THE SEA

There are few places in the world that ring with as much magic as the ocean. The Sasquatches are well aware of that magic and stand ready to reward all those who come hungry for inspiration to its shores. As a landlocked boy from the mountains, I was almost sixteen before I had my first real encounter with the sea. I found a piece of my soul there that I didn't even know I was missing. Ever since then, I have to feel the sand between my toes and smell the sweet, briny scent of the sea at least once a year.

When you're at the beach, everything is right with the world. I've found it's an excellent place to write, draw, dream, play, and discover. It changes every day, every hour, washing up new treasures and adventures. Need to hit your creative reset button?

The beach is an excellent place to do it.

#71. PLANT A GARDEN

No one can truly appreciate the value of a seed until he's planted a garden and watched it grow. My mother kept a garden when we were kids, and I always looked forward to and relished the harvest.

Peas, beans, berries, peppers, lettuce, tomatoes. If you haven't experienced the unique delight of a vine-ripened tomato, still warm from the sun, I daresay you probably haven't really lived.

Years ago for an art class in college, I created an art journal about the peas I had planted. I was a newlywed, living in a tiny apartment with no possibility of garden space. But I was a potter. So I made a hanging planter and planted six small seeds in the rich soil. As the seeds began to sprout and grow, I took notes, every day, of the progress the seeds were making. It was a beautiful experience, watching green life grow at eye level over the course of several weeks until I could harvest the peas and eat them. Out of six small seeds, dozens of beautiful, tasty pods had grown–each filled with several more seeds.

It's been said that every seed has an angel that bends over it and whispers, "Grow, grow." I believe the same must be true of every seed of talent and ability God has planted in our souls. Give that seed some decent water and a little sunlight, and it will begin to grow no matter how long it's been lying dormant. Nurture it, and it will produce joy and nourishment for you and everyone around you. And if you continue to tend the seed, it will multiply and bless more lives than you could ever imagine.

#72. GET OUT OF THE RUT

The power of the Sasquatches to jumpstart your creative life is limited, if not completely impeded, by the rut. Whether you're stuck in The Rut of Tradition; The Rut of Fear; The Rut of

Habit; The Rut of Comfort; or any other number of deep, fruitless ruts, no amount of encouragement or cajoling will enable you to make significant progress if you won't get out of the stinkin' rut!

And the inconvenient truth is that the only person who can rescue you from the rut is you.

If you've been coasting along in a rut for a while, you may have entirely forgotten that you actually have a choice. That's part of the rut's evil genius, blinding us to all other choices and alternative possibilities. The reasons for falling into ruts are as varied as the people who fall. And studies have shown that the only way out is to make a conscious decision to leave and then to refuse to go back or fall into any other ruts.

If you've spent any length of time in the rut, you'll soon discover that this new life—with its dusty roads full of multiple forks, speed bumps, and potholes—will probably feel daunting. This is normal for everyone who's ever pulled himself away from the strong grips of a rut. The rut's purpose has been and always will be to lull you into submission by keeping you comfortable and lethargic while, like a giant boa constrictor, it slowly squeezes out all of your resistance and promises to make all the difficult choices for you. But in the rut—without options and choices and the ability to choose your own adventure—your growth has been at least stunted if not altogether squelched. The reality of that doesn't sound very attractive, does it? You want out, don't you? Beware that the rut probably won't let you go easy. It likes holding people back from progression and opportunity.

If you push on and are able to sever the cords that have kept you down in the rut, you need to be aware that as you press forward, forging a new direction, the rut will call out to you, tempting you to remember the life of ease you'd been enjoying for so long. Many yield to that call, falling back into the rut even after they've tasted the sweet joys of freedom. It takes courage to leave the rut. It takes even more courage to not allow yourself to fall back in. But if you push on, you'll see that the less-traveled path will bring you through vibrant glens, stunning canyons, and magnificent woods to places of joy you could never have known if you'd stayed in the rut.

While the rut cries out, "Come back, it's scary out there!" remember that the rich joys of freedom, passion, and creativity can thrive only beyond the reach of the rut.

#73. EXPECT IT TO BE DIFFICULT

Yep, nothing about living a creative life is easy. It will require time and loads of effort. You will lose sleep and tears and probably a lot of hair and skin too. It's almost certain that your friends and family will call you crazy and you'll often feel lonely. There will be many times when you'll be tempted to give up. And many other times when you'll feel lost and confused. If you experience these things, know that it is all normal. If it were easy to follow your dreams, everyone would be doing it.

If you keep your senses open, you'll find many fellow travelers to help you along the way. Accept their encouragement. The Sasquatches, too, will hear your cries and toss you bones of creative solutions. But don't expect anybody to pick up your wagon and pull it for you. The wagon is all yours. You know where to go. When things feel dark, take time to be still. Open your journal and read how far you've come. There will probably always be easier ways to make a living, but none of them will be as fun and rewarding. Keep your chin up and your shoulder to the wheel.

#74. DON'T BELIEVE EVERYTHING YOU HEAR

You can find anything you're looking for on the internet. Some of it will be true. Some of it will not. No, rubbing lemons on your face will not allow you to go undetected by security cameras. Yes, Barack Obama was born in the USA. And despite what anybody says, there is definitely no African prince who wants to deposit $10,000,000 into your bank account so he can split it with you later.

The truth is, it's very easy to get excited, distracted, and/or derailed by falsehoods. You don't have time for it. Every minute you spend with a falsehood is a minute that is being stolen from your creative pursuits. Get busy so the next time you hear there's no such thing as a Sasquatch, you can not only set the record straight but also show the creative evidence to prove otherwise.

#75. YOUVE GOT TO KNOW WHEN TO HOLD EM, KNOW WHEN TO FOLD EM, KNOW WHEN TO WALK AWAY, KNOW WHEN TO RUN

Seducing a Sasquatch requires patience, endurance, and longevity. But it's also important to know when you're in over your head. Following the points listed in this field guide will enable you to avoid or overcome many of the mistakes commonly made by folks whose attempts at seduction fall short. But there is no field guide available that can prepare you completely for unforeseen traps, accidents, and derailments. If your ship runs aground, take the time to assess the damages. Get a second opinion. Maybe a third or fourth. If it's necessary to abandon ship, make sure to gather up the logbooks and all the other helpful materials and lessons before she sinks.

Take some time to regroup. Figure out what went wrong. Change course if necessary. And start again. Quitting is always an option but rarely, if ever, the best one. Experience can be very expensive, but it's a powerful teacher. Going down with the ship has never been good for anyone, but abandoning it while it can still be saved is wasteful. Only you will know if and when a project needs to be abandoned.

I don't know any successful person who hasn't had her share of challenges; problems; and, yes, failures. But the wise ones, the successful ones, know that you're not licked until you give up. Yes, getting out of the rut and choosing your own path is a gamble with uncertain jackpots and rewards. Listen to your heart, and you will know when to cut your losses or push on and endure.

#76. PROCEED AS THE WAY OPENS

This has become a constant theme in my own life. It's an old Quaker proverb that has reference to Jesus Christ–the way, the truth, and the light. As Christ opens the way for us, we must be willing to move our feet if we want ways to continue to open. Patience will be required as we wait for direction and for things to open up. Ways may open that we didn't anticipate, causing us some anxiety. Or they can confuse us by closing surprisingly and without warning. We won't always have answers or know the reasons why, but if we muster up the courage to always proceed as the way opens, our lives will turn out far better than we ever could have planned.

77. LEAVE ROOM FOR MAGIC

Some people believe in the power of setting goals, and they plan out their lives with such detail and precision that they don't leave any room for magic to happen. Being unwaveringly determined with our plans or our goals may ensure we reach them, but if we do it at the expense of discovering magic along the way, we might be shooting ourselves in the foot.

I learned this lesson early in my life. My goal was to be a student body officer (SBO). I ran every year from fifth to eleventh grade. I put myself out there, had good skits, and tried to make friends and buy whatever votes I could. When I got to high school, I was introduced to pottery. It was challenging and messy. My goal to be an SBO kept me running for office, and pottery was always the class I was planning to drop when I won so I could make room for the student government class. But I never won an election. Yep, I lost every time. I had a goal. It was a pretty good goal that would have helped me out in the scholarship arena. But it didn't turn out like I planned. And I thank God every day that it didn't. I would have missed out on so many levels of magic that shaped and influenced my life in endlessly meaningful ways. So set some goals for your life. Work hard to achieve them. But always remember that a wise a Seductioneer will leave room for the magic to surprise and delight him.

#78. LEARN TO IMPROVISE

Flexibility is an important key to finding success in any field. But if it's a creative field you're plowing, flexibility is especially crucial. Without it, you'll get stuck and waste a whole lot of time. Don't have the right tool? Improvise. Don't have the skill set you think you'll need? Improvise. The Sasquatches always favor the flexible who are willing to improvise their way through any mess that may arise. Without flexibility, you won't be any better off than a lonely stick in the mud.

Sasquatch doesn't allow his lack of a fishing pole to keep him from fishing.

#79. REMEMBER THAT LOVE IS THE GREATEST ART OF ALL

A Sasquatch will always warn those who take up his trail that if they do so at the expense of love, no success they may ever find will be worthwhile. Seducing the Sasquatch can be fun and rewarding on many levels. But love will always remain the greatest art of all. With love running through your veins and escaping your body with every breath, not only will you have the magic of the Sasquatches behind you, but all will be well in your life. Your priorities will fall into their proper order. And life will have not only meaning but also pleasure.

#80. BEWARE THAT FEAR IS THE RESULT OF THE SUM TOTAL OF ALL THE LIES YOU TELL YOURSELF

Sasquatches are sensitive to critical talk and lies of all sorts. So start telling yourself some truths! Just as darkness is chased away by the light, fear flees at the sight of truth and love. Whether you naturally tend to be self-critical and negative or only come to these attitudes when things are tough, stop it! Crumple up the sum total of the lies you've told yourself, and toss them away. And as you begin each new day moving forward, treat it like a blank sheet of paper that has endless possibilities as a receptacle for beauty and magic.

#81. FILL THE CARD CATALOG

Years ago I attended and presented at a workshop held for creative people in the printing industry.

I shared the program with a wonderful painter I had always admired–James C. Christensen. James was one of those Seductioneers who always inspired me with his seemingly endless curiosity and imagination. Even though that workshop took place nearly twenty years ago, I still remember many of the details he spoke about.

Projecting a slide of a card catalog (yeah, I know, two things that may be foreign words to a younger generation), he talked about how our minds are similar to Dewey's decimalized reference catalog with its many accessible file drawers. The trick, he suggested, was filling our card catalogs with images and ideas that could be drawn from at any time to create our own conglomeration of awesomeness. He talked about how he probably had the biggest beetle collection in the state and a vast collection of costumes, both of which he used for his incredible fantasy paintings.

I've observed that most people pass through their days nearly completely oblivious to the world around them. Distracted by their thoughts and more often their devices, most people don't look into the faces of those they pass on the street. They don't notice the way the grass grows through the cracks in the sidewalk or observe the subtle shadows that are cast by the peeling paint on the neighbor's garage. An artist notices details. Her eyes are open to changes, shapes, colors, and patterns. We can all develop the senses of an artist by consciously thinking about filling our card catalog. And then when we are looking for new ideas, we can draw on the vast library at our fingertips. Wherever you go, whoever you talk to, whatever you eat or smell or hear, take a piece of everything you experience and organize it in your card catalog. From the moment you open your eyes in the morning to when you close them at night, be hungry and anxious to take it all in. The Sasquatches suggest that you stop allowing your phone to rob you and your card catalog of the incredible images and experiences that are all around you. Put it away. Take it all in. Make memories that you can borrow from for the rest of your life.

#82. TAKE TIME TO DANCE

Before the beginning of recorded time, the Sasquatches discovered that life without a little boogie in it can be mighty boring. As we are reminded in the movie Footloose, even the Bible states that there is a time to dance. It's good for the body and the mind when you cut loose and express yourself through dance. The Sasquatches also learned that dancing gets blood flowing to the creative part of your brain and makes you smile.

Don't worry about lessons. No matter your age or ability, all it takes is a compelling tune. Turn up the volume, and let your inner weirdo dance like

she's alone in the woods. Or, for an even better time, invite your friends to join you. It will likely require you to forget about your resistance to vulnerability. That's a good thing! And you will likely have people give you strange looks. It's good practice. When you pursue a creative life, it's pretty much a rule that you're gonna get a lot of strange looks. Don't worry—it's only the look of envy.

#83. GET PAST THE NOES

Before I headed off to college for the first time, my father thought it would be a really good idea for me to have some door-to-door sales experience. I reluctantly complied after I heard a pep talk from one of the top World Book Encyclopedia salesmen, who bragged about easy money. I committed to giving it one month.

From my very first day to the last day of that very long month, it sucked—bad. Word on the street was that this crazy thing called the Internet was coming soon to a neighborhood nearby and encyclopedias would soon be obsolete. I got a whole lot of noes. But every day, I'd dress up, get on my motor scooter, and drive through neighborhoods until I could muster up the guts to start knocking doors.

My father, who'd spent a couple of summers in college selling books door to door, told me that all I had to do was to get through the noes and I would be able to find all sorts of people who'd be anxious to say yes. I don't know if it was my product; my approach; or the price of my leather-bound, gilded books that would soon be defunct, but I was able to convince only one customer to buy a set of encyclopedias.

The experience wasn't a total waste. In fact, it was one I've reflected on many times over the last twenty-five years. I've never been tempted again to trade significant discomfort and anxiety for the promise of easy money. Real money, as it turns out, is rarely easy. But the reality that we all have to get through the noes remains a vital truth. Whatever you do in life, you will likely face a wall—or at least a fence—of noes. Many people give up before they get to the end of the negatories. It's hard to keep your chin up when all you ever hear is no. But the folks who make it through the noes are the ones who get to do and be what they want when they grow up. Disney will never tell you this, but the only road to Happily Ever After cuts through the dark, haunted forest of Youvogottabekiddinme and across the bridgeless river made up of nothing but blood, sweat, and tears.

Can't handle the negativity or the difficult odds? Don't worry. There are plenty of jobs that won't require the time and torment. But beware that most of those will require you to check your dreams, and maybe your soul, at the door. If you'll consult a Sasquatch, he'll always tell you that the noes, though they may seem scary with their horns and fangs, are really more for show rather than posing any real threat. Their main job is to keep the fainthearted out of the world of yeses. Yes, the yeses do exist. But they are always on the other side of the wall of noes. And just because you get one good yes, you shouldn't assume that you're home free. If you're on the path of creativity, there will always be noes growing like brambles across your path, trying to trip you up and keep you discouraged. Press on. Get to the yeses.

#84. PAY YOUR DUES ASAP

Pablo Picasso is widely known as one of the most prolific artists who ever lived. Primarily a painter, he also experimented with sculpture, ceramics, and printmaking, producing thousands upon thousands of works of art over his lifetime. He was one of the rare visual artists who became a millionaire long before his death.

How did he do it? Well, among other things, he paid his dues early. Picasso said that in order to become an artist, you have to paint a thousand paintings. Malcolm Gladwell suggests something similar with his ten-thousand-hour requirement for someone to become an expert.

A few years back, I met a woman at a workshop where I was a presenter. About halfway through my presentation, she got up and excused herself, saying she had to get to something. I thought it was a little rude and certainly odd that she hadn't planned things better. A couple of weeks later, this same woman dropped by my studio to thank me for what I'd said. I was a little surprised because she'd only heard the half of it. After apologizing, she explained that she'd set a goal of painting one painting every day for a year. She'd kept her goal for several months but had been stumped that day, wondering what to paint. Something I'd said gave her the vision she'd been waiting for, and she didn't want to delay. She wanted to pay her dues so she could get to the next level, and she couldn't allow a little thing like a workshop to get in her way.

No matter what you choose, it's gonna take time. You won't be an expert in the first month, the first year, or maybe not even the first decade. Success belongs to those with patience, a hardy work ethic, and longevity. But the sooner you pay your dues, the sooner you'll be reaching your goals and enjoying the benefits of your hard work. I'm often asked for advice about following one's dreams. Invariably, my response includes the critical need for both hard work and patience. Every Sasquatch I've ever met believes that if you're not willing or able to commit to both, you might consider a different career.

#85. BE AS KIND A POSSIBLE

You might wonder what kindness has to do with creativity. Kindness is in fact and deed one of the best kept secrets of creativity. Why? Well, as the very essence of greatness, kindness is a virtue beyond comparison. It inspires the giver to open his heart and offer a portion of love. It inspires recipients to open their hearts and receive it.

Kindness often costs nothing to give, yet it adds immense value to all interactionsand relationships.

If you're feeling a little undercreative, any Sasquatch would suggest that offering a little kindness will go a long way to jump-starting your cold heart and getting things rolling again. And the cool thing about kindness is that more often than not, it's contagious. Want to change the outlook of an entire community or nation? Start with kindness, and watch how creative acts of service, love, and compassion ripple through the hearts and minds of all who are touched by it.

Our world today is struggling with a kindness deficit. You can help by giving a piece of yourself to another through a selfless act of kindness. It starts with a smile but has no limits.

#86. BUT DONT BE A DOORMAT

Along your way, you will likely encounter people who are dead in the kindness department. If you're up to a challenge, it's often possible to revive such an individual through regular and sincere acts of kindness. But it's also possible, despite all your good intentions, for you to become a doormat, getting sucked into the vortex of negativity. Ain't nobody got time for that.

The Sasquatches wish to remind you that the sage old adage "if at first you don't succeed, well…so much for skydiving" certainly applies here. Your life and your psyche are too valuable to be consumed by any manner of darkness. Sometimes walking away is the only responsible thing to do. All mortal love has its limits. Don't be ashamed if you reach yours. Move on to greener pastures where your efforts can be better appreciated and make the difference you hope for.

#87. DONT LET YOUR CRITICS WIN

The sad truth is that haters are always gonna hate. But the happy truth is that you don't have to listen to them. I was shocked when, a month before my first book was even published, someone reviewed it on Goodreads. Somehow they had gotten a copy of an early manuscript from a distant friend of a friend and decided to post a review. It was not nice. I was upset. The reviewer suggested that I should just keep making pottery and give up on writing. I stewed in those unkind juices for a week or better. Several things had changed in later rewrites, but that didn't matter. Her review was out there. And it hurt.

Before my father had ever read anything I had ever written, he suggested with harsh words that I was wasting my time. That kept me from writing for over a year. I let him win. I'm still sad that I let him affect me that way—that I wasted so much time on something so negative and ignorant. But I learned my lesson that first time, and though it still hurt when it happened a second time, I wasn't about to let the unknown critic win. By far the majority of the reviews of my books have been positive, but in the beginning, it was the rare negative one that sucked up my chi and left me feeling angry and depressed. In recent years, I've decided to do exactly what so many other writers and artists have learned works best when confronted with negative or hostile critics: ignore them.

After receiving that first negative review, I spent a little bit of time on Goodreads looking at reviews of many different books. I realized they were all over the board. You can't possibly make everyone happy, nor should you want to. One of my favorite books, The Alchemist, an international best seller, has an average of only three stars with plenty of nasty reviews. But Paulo Coelho and thousands of other authors with negative reviews continue to follow their passions and their muses.

I have since renamed Goodreads DisgruntledEnglishMajors. It's a sad truth that many people, when they want to do something but either get stymied or delayed in their progress, instead of redoubling their efforts and trying again, turn instead into the loudest critics of those who actually accomplish that which they set out to do. Don't let them win. The light and love you have to offer this world is too valuable to be hampered or shelved by the ignorant haters who've lost their own hopes and dreams and are bent on making others miserable too. Don't let them.

#88. LIMIT YOUR INHALATION TO WHATS NECESSARY

After hateful critics, one of the next most dangerous animals in the jungle is praise. Though intentions of exuberant fans are usually positive-and their accolades often feel good to the ego-inhaling them too deeply can be equally damaging, causing one to rest on his laurels rather than getting back to work. Pride is an interesting vice. We all need a little to keep us going, but the Sasquatches always warn that too much of it can be incredibly destructive. How much is too much? It'll be different for everyone. But if you find yourself more concerned about how many likes you have than you are about pushing forward with the next creative idea, chances are you're way past the safe threshold. Back it up. Spit it out. Do your best work. And stop worrying what people will think of it. That's not why you're doing this, remember? You chose this path because you knew you couldn't be happy doing anything else. And as soon as you're with your project, move on to the next one.

#89. THE NEXT ONE WILL BE YOUR BEST ONE YET

Yep, and the one after that will be even than that. And the one after that… Well, you get the picture. Why stop now when you've got more creative ground to cover. One-hit wonders are certainly happier than no-hit floppers, but you still got magic in you, right? Put it to work. You know what it took to learn that first language of creative success. The second language will come easier, and the third will come easier still. Don't waste the momentum by giving up or taking a break. Fans are waiting to see, hear, read, and experience your next masterpiece. Don't make them wait. People die every day. Don't deny them the opportunity to love your next baby too.

#90. DONT HESITATE TO ASK FOR HELP

If you come to a fork in the road and don't know which one to take, ask. If you're stuck on a persistent problem, ask. If you've worked yourself into a corner and are not sure which way is out—or even up—ask. You are never alone in the trials that keep you from progression. Consult an expert. Talk to a friend. Pray for guidance.* Don't let your pride or your fear of losing likes slow your progress. There's no shame in asking for help, but the same cannot be said of giving up or getting lost because you were unwilling or scared to ask for help. *Though expert opinion varies wildly, studies have shown that it may be most effective to do this one first.

#91. BE RESILIENT

I like to define resilience as the ability to bounce. Heaven knows we're all gonna fall. That's just a part of life we don't get to choose. But fortunately we do get to choose how high we'll bounce. Maintaining a positive attitude and choosing to be flexible with our goals will allow us to bounce much higher than we would if we were unyielding and stubborn.

Children are by nature incredibly resilient. Thank goodness they are, or we'd all be doomed to lives of depression. What's happened to you since your childhood will likely affect the height of your bounce, but we each get to decide how much of our history is allowed to play a role in our present and future lives. Any help the Sasquatches can offer you will be limited by how much of that history, both good and bad, you cling to. If you're interested in a better future, you've got to be able to treat your history as apple farmers treat their less-than-perfect fruit—squeeze it to take what's tasty and valuable, and throw the rest of it into the compost so it can foster the growth of next year's apples. They've learned by sad experience that hanging onto the harvest's bruised apples only spoils the good ones. Bounce high and prosper.

#92. BUILD A COMMUNITY

Tolkien and Lewis had the Inklings. Benjamin Franklin and his friends had the Junto. The Beatles had…well…the other Beatles. Creative people feed on each other to produce more creativity. The Sasquatches have long known that creative progress rarely if ever happens in a vacuum—except maybe ideas about vacuums. We need each other. If you can't find a group, start one.

Lynnette and I were invited to join an intimate fledgling poetry group a few years ago. It's been delightful, educational, and meaningful to share vulnerable moments, laughter, and tears as we've listened to each other's poetry. It is unlikely that I ever would have written my book of collected poems, The Lost Art of Wooing Rabbits and Other Wild Hares, without their influence, encouragement, and input.

Cooking clubs, bowling clubs, bands, artists cooperatives, and synchronized doubles tennis groups could offer you the community support you've been craving. Creative people are often quirky people, but they're very often friendly and outgoing. Invite them into your home and heart. Break bread together, and creative ideas will flow naturally.

#93. BE A CHEERLEADER

The creative world needs more cheerleaders. And Sasquatches, with their mangy fur and rugged scent, often have limited access to the public. But you on the other hand can fulfill the needs of many who need an enthusiatic shot in the arm. Be sincere but also generous with your praise and encouragement. Without his brother Theo, Vincent Van Gogh would have undoubtedly been even more discouraged. Sometimes a good word is all that stands between a creative soul pressing on through the hard times and giving up completely. You have it in you to change a life through championing the work or cause of another. Selfishly holding back praise and boosterism can slow the progress and confidence of the talented yet insecure, thus hurting the entire world. Open your heart. Open your mouth. Change the world.

#94. GET PAST YOUR BLUE PERIOD

Before Picasso became Picasso, he went through what critics and biographers termed his Blue Period. It was a time when he was figuring out his emotions, his style, his goals. It seems like all artists and creative people go through such a time. It can last for months or even decades before the artist hatches from her cocoon and spreads her wings. The work produced during this time is often not very good, but it's important for the ultimate direction and understanding that will come through it.

When I first got started making pottery full-time, I went through a yearlong blue period. I was making a lot of work, but none of it I could say was all mine as I borrowed ideas and forms from teachers and creative mentors. And I wasn't as skilled as I wanted to be with making my forms and, especially, with my glazing. I made a lot of brown and orange pots. They were the nicest pots I could have produced at the time, but they were boring and common and totally not exciting or fun. I needed to find my own creative voice and figure out how to express it.

Through allowing myself time to play, make mistakes, and express my unique personality, my pots began evolving. Browns and oranges gave way to brighter, happier glazes in all the colors. I stretched myself, experimenting in processes and textures. I broke some rules, mixed in some advice I'd learned from other potters, spent a lot of time dancing with the Sasquatches, filled several sketchbooks with doodles and ideas, and ultimately found myself and my voice.

Your blue period may be painful and unpleasant like it is for most creatives. Move through it quickly. Learn all that you can about yourself, your materials, and your process so you can move on to the good stuff, the stuff that makes you happy, the stuff that is all you.

#95. BECOME A NET PRODUCER OF HAPPINESS

Just as a country's trade balance tips into imbalance when its imports outweigh its exports, we become imbalanced if we consume joy but do nothing to create it. Sasquatches throughout the world revel in encouraging people who are doing all they can to maintain balance of any kind. They become even more excited when they see someone doing his or her best to become a net producer of joy. By exercising creativity of almost every kind, you're not only producing joy, but you're also inspiring others to do the same.

Should you ever find yourself feeling blue, it's likely that there's a happiness imbalance somewhere in your life. Contrary to common beliefs and practice, selfishly pigging out on or hoarding happiness and joy does nothing to make you any happier. Why? Because joy and happiness must be shared in order for the full measure of their creation to be realized. Pig out on them, and you become an unhappy glutton. Hoard them, and they will only shrivel and die. But conversely, sharing happiness multiplies it exponentially across time and space. By becoming a net producer of happiness, you commit to trading your natural propensities toward selfishness and self-indulgence for a life of optimism, cheerfulness, and joy-filled service.

Like anything else of any real, lasting value, becoming a net producer requires work. This change of direction and focus often feels daunting to many who begin this path, but I promise that your efforts will be rewarded as the Sasquatches of balance, joy, and creativity shower you with their unequivocal and incomparable gifts.

#96. DARE TO COLOR OUTSIDE THE LINES

Since the time you picked up your first crayon, you have been told to color inside the lines. The Sasquatches rebel against all sorts of confinement because they know that real magic usually takes place only when you push beyond the imaginary lines of confinement, along the table, across the floor, and out the front door. And once you're out of the house, you might as well keep going—all the way down the street, gathering momentum as you roll. And at some point, if you keep the momentum going, you'll discover that you're not rolling at all but actually flying.

Your dreams are too big to be defined by someone else's lines and borders. If they're not too big, they could be. Break away from the cute coloring books filled with black-lined pictures everyone else is coloring. A sketchbook full of blank pages is all you need to dream of what can be.

#97. SIMPLIFY

When we refinished our home a few years back, we added over five hundred square feet of handmade tile. I created all of the tiles–ranging in size from one square inch to twelve square inches–in a huge range of colors and textures. One of the very last tiles I installed, and the one that gets the most attention and comments when people tour our home, is a tile that reads, "Simplify." It's advice I think about often but rarely take. I'm an artist. I like details. I like color. I like the passion and creativity that come with those things and that so often enhance my art.

Simplified yoga by the lake.

But many details of our lives hold us back. The drive for the acquisition of stuff and then the care and storage of that stuff very often complicate things and distract us from living creative, meaningful, simple lives. Overscheduling our children's lives with music lessons, dance, and sports can sap their budding creativity and teach them to believe they have to be überbusy in order to be successful and happy. We rob them of the creative, self-actuated play that occurs naturally in all healthy children.

Since the dawning of the digital age, children have also been robbed of their creative natures by the screens we put in front of them. Most kids wouldn't know what to do with the duct tape and cardboard boxes we used as children to fuel our own dreams and imagination. Instead, they are falling into the unprofitable and egocentric trap of immediate gratification.

We need to stop the glorification of busy and recognize that many of the greatest joys in life come from slowing down, looking around, and truly experiencing the world around us rather than constantly trying to escape into a virtual parallel world. One of the perils of this virtual world is that it's already been created, down to the minutest of details. It may be exciting and beautiful and glossy, but it doesn't require us to think or do anything. Rather, it lulls and dulls us into a sense of comfort and complacency.

The process of simplification is not passive. It requires action, conscious thought, and prioritization. We probably all know people who have decided to push back against the digital era by not getting cell phones or denying them to their children. In some ways, I see this as admirable. But in other ways, it looks like a child trying to prevent the rising tide from devouring his sandcastle.

We are surrounded by extremes in our world today. Perhaps we even embrace many of them ourselves. I believe the best and most practical way of simplifying our lives is to adopt the ancient and oft-neglected concept and practice of moderation. By being moderate, we exercise self-control and self-discipline. We prioritize, knowing we can't possibly do it all. We thoughtfully consider how we use our time, our talents, and our resources. We allow ourselves to cut out the things that really don't matter to make way for more of the things, people, and experiences that do. And as we do so, we make room in our lives for the Sasquatches to inspire us. Don't justify—simplify.

#98. PICK YOUR BATTLES

For most of us, a good life requires us to fight for it. But the Sasquatches are sick and tired of competing for the attention of would-be creatives who are distracted either by wars they can't win or battles that aren't worth fighting. We only have so many hours in the day. Focus your attention and energies on the things worth fighting for, and then you'll have just enough time to focus on the creative things that matter most.

#99. BE PASSIONATELY CURIOUS

"I have no special talents. I am only passionately curious," Einstein admitted. Curiosity is the common thread that runs through the lives of every great explorer, scientist, and artist the world has ever known. It is the seed of all awesomeness. It keeps men and women, boys and girls asking questions and searching for answers. It enables us to build towers to the sky while also finding the answers to the smallest details of our genetic code.

A Sasquatch himself is a curiosity. And dedicating your life to his seduction—becoming a Seductioneer—will ensure that your curiosity will continue to grow bright. Never stop asking why or how. In fact, question everything. But don't just question like a toddler who asks a million whys a day but never really listens to the answers. Question, and let the answers lead to more questions and more answers. Then share what you learn with others, encouraging your curiosity to become contagious. Infinite numbers of answers are yet to be found or discovered. And many of them have been waiting patiently just for you to discover them.

#100. DONT JUST EXIST - LIVE; DONT JUST LIVE - THRIVE

Besides being covered in hair, the Sasquatch and the grizzly bear have at least one other thing in common—they are repulsed by dead people. This is good to know if you're trying to avoid being mauled by a bear. But playing dead will do you little good if you're trying to seduce a Sasquatch. As Benjamin Franklin so aptly noted, "Many people die at twenty-five and aren't buried until they are seventy-five."

Not developing creativity in the first place and not keeping it nourished throughout your lifetime will surely bring on the signs of early death. It's not enough to breathe and take up space to prove we're alive. We were born to create, to imagine, to do cool stuff, to be awesome! We're not here to languish in boredom and mediocrity until old age finally strips us of our last vestiges of life. No, we're here to prosper and flourish.

So, how are you doing? Are you thriving? Are you flourishing? Are you smarter, wiser, more creative today than you were yesterday? Could your battery use a recharge? Could your systems benefit from a jump start? An overhaul? A complete and total makeover?

Only you can decide to make the change. You decide whether to allow the Sasquatches to influence your life, and you choose how much influence you'll let them have. Only you can decide if you will thrive. Choosing to thrive will require significantly more effort than mere existence, but the payback is guaranteed to be well worth it. Choose to thrive. Choose to make your life exciting, brilliant, and memorable. Strive to leave a legacy that will inspire your children and grandchildren to stand tall, work hard, and resist accusations of being common or ordinary.

#101. TRUST YOUR HEART

If you can't trust your own heart, there ain't nobody you can trust. Trusting your heart will help you when the road ahead is dark. It will help you when you're tempted to give up. Don't give up!

The Sasquatches will always be there to inspire if you're willing to listen and work, but knowing and trusting your own heart will be necessary as you incorporate all your creative ideas and put them into practice. You will make plenty of mistakes and false turns as you progress. Don't worry. That's part of the process. But you were born to be a Seductioneer. You were born to stand out. You were born to be you! And you will never be satisfied and content until you have fulfilled the measure of your creation. So stop putting it off. Step away from the easy chair. Live the life you've been hoping for. Trust that your heart will never lead you astray.

God left the world unfinished for man to work his skill upon. He left the electricity in the cloud, the oil in the earth. He left the rivers unbridged and the forests unfelled and the cities unbuilt. God gives to man the challenge of raw materials, not the ease of finished things.

He leaves the pictures unpainted and the music unsung and the problems unsolved, that man might know the joys and glories of creation."

-Thomas S Monson

ABENDMAHL PRESS

Personalized books can be ordered
at www.potterboy.com.
There, you can register for the email mailing list
to receive updates about upcoming books, shows, and events.

Ben enjoys hearing from his readers.
You can reach him at benbehunin@comcast.net
or through snail mail at:

Abendmahl Press
P.O Box 581083
Salt Lake City, Utah 84158-1083

For speaking engagements including
book clubs, funerals and bar mitzvahs
call 801-883-0146

See the short video Quin Boardman created about Ben at
www.hiveseries.com

For design information, contact
Bert Compton at bert@comptonds.com

benbehunin

niederbippboy

EX LIBRIS
Donegan

How to Seduce a Sasquatch

First printing, January 2018

Published by
Abendmahl Press
P.O. Box 581083
Salt Lake City, Utah 84158-1083

ISBN 978-0-9998516-8-5

Photography Ben Behunin, Bert Compton
Designed by Ben Behunin and Bert Compton
Layout by Bert Compton

OTHER BOOKS BY BEN BEHUNIN

Remembering Isaac
Discovering Isaac
Becoming Isaac
Forget-Me-Notes
Borrowing Fire
Put A Cherry On Top
The Lost Art of Wooing Rabbits and Other Wild Hares
The Disciple of the Wind

Ben's books are available from his website, www.potterboy.com, www.amazon.com and wherever above average books are sold.

seduce

(si-doos, -dyoos), *verb*

1. to attract powerfully

Sasquatch

(sas-kwoch, -kwach), *noun*

1. those doggone creative but sometimes masterfully elusive muses we chase through wood and glen, hoping to catch.
2. another term for Bigfoot

A THEORETICAL FIELD GUIDE

How to Seduce a SASQUATCH

THEORIES

Behind the Practical Seduction of

CREATIVITY

Introduction

Hello, and welcome to Sasquatch Seduction 101.

If you're here and think you're in the right place, welcome.

If you picked up this book by accident, you can probably still put it back where you found it and no one will get hurt.

If you picked it up by accident but you're curious, that may be a good enough reason to hold onto it.

Whatever the case may be, we welcome you to this loose association of creative Seductioneers

Never heard of us?

Don't worry. You're not the first. Even though we've been around since the dawn of time, many people have lived their whole lives without knowing, or knowing that they know, a Seductioneer. Others have been practicing this art/science/magic hybrid for many years without ever fully being aware of the gifts and talents they possess. Still others, when they become aware of the unique, creative superpowers available to them through the study of and adherence to the founding principles of Seductioneerism, are anxious to learn more.

For this reason and many more that will be discussed throughout this textbook and its accompanying field guide, we are excited to share with you the accumulated knowledge and understanding of this often misunderstood discipline.

Although the attempt to define the term Seductioneer flies in the face of Seductioneers' general desires to remain undefined and free of restrictive banners, with great sensitivity I offer only a basic and generalized characterization in the hopes of offering some sense of understanding.

seductioneer

(si-**duhk**-sh*uh*-neer), *noun*

1. A member of a loosely associated group of artistic/creative weirdos who believe innovative ideas can be and often are gifts that come as a result of affiliating with Sasquatches. Seductioneers tend to be unique individuals who are uninterested in conforming to "normal" or "common" behaviors, practices, and patterns, choosing instead to march to the beat of their own drummer in the hopes of discovering inventive, originative, or ingenious answers to life's most difficult questions.

Over the course of the last two decades, I have often been asked to further outline the characteristics of a Seductioneer. I generally shy away from attempting to do so as I recognize that by our very nature and design we typically loathe being clumped together within strict lines, borders, or boundaries. That being said, I will attempt to share some common attributes that I have observed over the years.

Seductioneers are:

- often considered enigmatic by their family and friends
- generally a happy lot
- passionately curious
- often classified as rebels and freethinkers
- historically the first people to be rounded up and sent away when conquering powers come to town
- typically eccentric
- celebrators of the beauty and singularity of individualism
- often manic and sometimes depressive
- typically quick to smile
- perpetually restless

- prone to insatiable creative itches
- inclined to sleep substantially less than the average human
- known to work hard and play even harder
- highly allergic to stale and stagnant places, individuals, and ideas
- generally excited about traveling and tend to do so often
- likely to question everything but generally focus their questioning on traditions, rituals, policies, politics, discrimination, and small ideas
- generally against allowing money to influence their decisions to choose the less-traveled road
- often thrifty but are inclined to be generous
- predisposed to be thoughtful
- often opinionated
- sometimes given to hyperbole
- appreciators of good stories and are often known to tell them
- inclined to surround themselves with beautiful things
- known to travel well in small packs but are often most at home in solitude
- opposed to coloring, thinking, or living inside boxes, lines, and borders
- typically dreamers, of both the day and night varieties
- idealists and pacifist
- collectors of friends, books, and art
- sometimes inclined not to care much about matching their clothes, socks or associates
- always ready for an adventure
- passionate about everything they do
- hate wasting time
- known to not have TVs
- more game to play sports than to view them
- often forgetful to eat when they're in the throes of creating
- expressive and crazy and would rather die than be tamed

Does this sound familiar? It should. You'd have to be either blind or at least unobservant to not have recognized these qualities in the lives of those around you. Perhaps you call such people friends. Perhaps you call them weirdos. Perhaps many of these things sound like you. Whatever the case may be, I'd be willing to bet you've had at least a secret desire to run with the Seductioneers. Whether you envy them, are scared of them, or would love to spend more time with them, this book will hopefully help you understand them better.

The elusive Sasquatch on the lookout for Seductioneers.

Since the dawn of the digital age, we the members of the International Sasquatch Seduction Society (I.S.S.S.), generally just referred to as Seductioneers, have noticed a steady decline in interest for the old ways. Kids these days just don't seem to want to get their hands dirty or even venture outdoors. We hope your desire to be involved may lead you down the path of creativity and allow you to discover for yourself the value of the vanishing art of Sasquatch seduction.

We at the I.S.S.S. fear that the complete loss of this ancient

wisdom and practice will doom the world—and thereby possibly the entire universe—to a state of complete and total lifeless and colorless mediocrity. Around the world, our Apathy and Stagnation Meters (AASMs) have been sounding a blaring alarm for nearly a decade, and they're only getting louder. Meanwhile, the native breeding grounds of the elusive, wild Sasquatches are being consumed by the rampant and thoughtless spread of strip malls and parking lots, forcing the lowly Sasquatches to retreat even deeper into the hinterlands.

Something has to be done!

With the purchase of this book, you have been officially deputized as a Sasquatch Seductioneer. Full induction into the I.S.S.S. will be available to you upon your completion of this course and after a swearing-in ceremony, whereupon you will be able to upgrade your sticker badge for a real one.

In this class, and through its accompanying Sasquatch Seduction Field Guide, we will explore some of the philosophies associated with the dying art of Sasquatch Seduction. For the past forty years, I've been studying this art, first as a curious young boy, later as an apprentice Seductioneer, and for the past twenty-two years as a bona fide member of the I.S.S.S. I have led countless expeditions into the wilds, trying to draw out the elusive Sasquatches from their caves, dens, and fortresses, where most have sequestered themselves, tired of being neglected and forgotten.

To date, we have spotted, photographed, and identified thousands of Sasquatches. Many have even become friends. They come to dinner from time to time when they're in the neighborhood. We try to always set a place at the table for the hungry wanderers and keep a warm place at the hearth for them to stop in and share a tale or unfold the secrets of the universe to which they hold celebrated keys. And if we're lucky, we rendezvous in quiet and wild places as often as time permits and opportunities arise.

As we visit together, my friends the Sasquatches, often complain about the lack of hospitality and respect they've been receiving over the last few decades. Fewer and fewer humans have been inviting them in to share a meal. Fewer and fewer humans are wandering out into the hinterlands. And even when they do wander into Sasquatch country, an increasing number are going solely for the purpose of acquiring selfies in hopes of enhancing their personae on social media. Fewer and fewer campfires dot the landscape after dusk, enticing fewer Sasquatches to visit and share their mysteries and their creative solutions to all the world's challenges.

For these reasons and many more, the I.S.S.S. along with the I.C.U.S.F.C. (to be discussed later) have commissioned me and my internationally acclaimed photographer friend and comrade, Harry von Lederhösen, to become ambassadors and create a course that might open the way for more frequent and higher-quality human/Sasquatch interactions and relations.

Our friends the Sasquatches, envision a world:

- where the wisdom of the Sasquatches is not chased back into the wilderness by the shotgun of lesser things
- where humans and Sasquatches can work together to find creative solutions to all the world's conundrums
- that is more colorful, hopeful, loving, and generous
- where peace is more important than power
- where people can come together instead of pulling apart
- without artificial walls, borders, or boundaries of any kind
- where mankind will choose to invoke the power of brotherly love rather than of hate or greed or selfishness

In short, they envision a much happier world.

Sound too good to be true?

Yeah, well, we get that a lot. But if we don't try, we'll never know

what we can do together. Yes, you could say the Sasquatches are a bold and happy band of idealists—idealists who know that the fulfillment of their vision can be realized only with the enlistment of thousands of believers, helpers, and, yes, Seductioneers.

This book is an invitation to come and join the revolution.

It's time to stop the assassination and neglect of the lowly Sasquatches. It's time to embrace our furry friends—to stoke the campfires of creativity, encouraging them to burn brighter and brighter that we might attract others who are hiding in the cold, sullen shadows. It's time to act before it's too late.

The majestic Sasquatch awaits those who act.

So, wait, how is a book like this going to help?

Well, I suppose there's no guarantee that it will.

Whether this book helps you in either your own creative endeavors or in supporting or understanding a creative friend or loved one—it's all up to you. There are a few books out there about creativity, but none of them have been written by a bona fide Seductioneer.

The seed for this book sat dormant in my brain for nearly two decades and finally began germinating soon after I began my pottery career twenty-two years ago. The germination process was triggered—as most germination is—by a question. Since that time, I've been asked the very same question probably close to a million times. And with each asking, the seed has grown a little bit more, sending out roots and leaves and branches.

It's hard to ignore a tree that's growing in the space between your ears. Fearing that the sapling would either split my head wide open or become root-bound and its growth be perilously hampered, I knew it needed more space to grow than the confines of my skull would allow.

Over these past twenty-two years, when people have found out I'm an artist, I've gotten a lot of questions. After the questioners have pinched me—I can only assume out of a desire to see if I'm real—and the initial shock of meeting a living, breathing artist has subsided, I can usually see the wheels in their heads turning slowly as they take in my art or see my name on my eight published books. This is especially true when folks come to my studio or tour our home for the first time during one of our semiannual open houses. They see the whimsical world we've created, see the shelves full of pots in a variety of colors, textures, and designs. They see people buying my books and coming back for more to introduce them to friends and loved ones. Inevitably the question comes,

"Where do you get all your ideas?"

I've discovered over the past twenty-two years that most people aren't looking for the long answer. They usually look at me goofy when I begin at age four with the story my grandfather—the first Seductioneer I ever met—told me about seducing a Sasquatch one winter while traversing through the woods near Yellowstone on the very snowshoes that hung above us on the wall of his A-frame cabin.

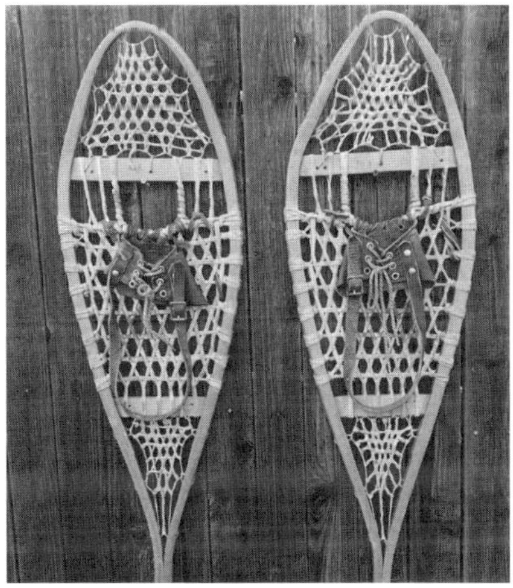

Grandpa's cabin and snowshoes.

No, I've learned that giving someone that answer is a little bit like giving them your entire medical history when they ask how you're doing—their eyes usually glaze over after the first ten seconds. People no longer have attention spans for such stories.

I've heard, in fact, that the average attention span for an American adult is currently 8.25 seconds and growing ever shorter. The average attention span for a goldfish is 9 seconds. Not a very hopeful comparison, right?

So, thus the book. Most people, no matter how curious they start out, decide to just let the mystery be if they've got to read a book to get an answer. It's too much work and requires too much attention. So with that information, I surmise that of the ten people who'll buy my book, maybe five will ever read it. I suppose it's kind of a bummer to put so

much time and effort into something few people will ever see. Come to think of it, it's probably pretty similar to the odds of a baby sea turtle hatching, making it to the sea, growing to adulthood, and coming back to the same beach to lay its own eggs.

But maybe that's enough. Maybe it's enough to lay two hundred eggs on a tropical beach by moonlight. After all, I'm not after the money. If I were, I would have chosen a much different path twenty-two years ago. My only real motivation for sharing my knowledge of the Sasquatches and the sources of my creative ideas is and always has been to help inspire and motivate individuals to think and act a little bigger.

Why do you even care?

Because I believe we're all capable of more. Whether it be more creativity, more patience, more awesomeness, or more ______________________ [fill in the blank].

But I believe all of that more requires not only conscious thought and drive but also a lot of work. Dreams are important, but without the work to make them real, they are little more than Potemkin villages.

My hopes are that with this book and a little help from the Sasquatches, you won't only learn where I get my ideas from, but you'll be able to get a whole bunch of ideas of your own. I'm interested in cutting out the middleman and sending you directly to the source. The Sasquatches really work best that way. They don't like the distractions they have to deal with when they're trying to get your attention. That's why they're most active in quiet places, removed from the babble and chaos of our noisy world. But as I mentioned before, such places are becoming increasingly difficult to find. In the name of progress, the native roaming grounds of the Sasquatches are being paved over to make room for a tamer, calmer, and more refined future.

The problem with a future that's been refined is that unfortunately

it often means it has also been defined, cutting out possibilities and drawing lines around what is in and what is out. Laurel Thatcher Ulrich, the Pulitzer Prize–winning Harvard professor, recognized the problems of a defined life when she said,

"Well-behaved women seldom make history."

But why stop with women? The same is certainly true for men, boys, and girls. Well-behaved generally is a term with strict definitions. It suggests borders and lines of delineation. It implies that if we color inside the lines and don't speak up or make a stir, all will be well. But will it? Will we ever fulfill the measure of our creation if we're held back by tradition, rituals, or the etiquette rules that have been deemed acceptable by prior generations and imposed upon us without any thought as to how they might dampen and impede our progress?

If we're ever going to follow our dreams and passions as far as they might take us, it seems quite certain we won't be able to honor all the barriers and parameters imposed upon us by others. There are many tried-and-true ways of creatively working around many if not all of these imposed obstacles. Protests and pep rallies, for example, are certainly employed by many, with mixed results. I personally prefer the Underground Railroad approach—keeping my head below the radar and just doing what I know I need to be doing. I've found this to be an even more effective use of my time and efforts than trying to start revolutions—at least loud ones.

Many who join the loud, vocal protests for their causes are likely to find a community of like-minded individuals, which can be a strength and rich support. But you may have also noticed that many of these protests that begin with noble intentions develop into chaos and lead to a mob mentality that is often ineffective and sometimes even counterproductive.

Those who choose the Underground Railroad approach are sometimes accused of being too passive. Those who choose this

technique may never enjoy similar camaraderie as those in a protest movement. They may in fact even feel lonely at times. They may miss the limelight and never be catapulted into the history books as martyrs for their cause. But while others are busy fighting battles they may never win, simply keeping one's nose to the grindstone and being true to one's inner voice can go a long way to achieving triumph in the battles that *can* be won.

I recognize that working alone has many benefits that those who work in groups never experience. For one, the agility and flexibility I have in making decisions could never be matched in working with a group. As a committee of one—sometimes two if I include my wife in the big decisions—I/we can move at comparatively lightning speed.

People who work together in groups or communities often discover that moving forward is slow and cumbersome. Good, vibrant ideas, when met with too many opinionated heads and voices, are too often harangued and debated into oblivion. I call this Death By Committee. It happens everyday in boardrooms around the world. Pursuing a creative life on your own enables you to avoid these landmines and pitfalls. If your idea is good, just, and successful, you will find that others will be inspired to push on with their own impassioned causes, inspiring revolutions of all shapes and sizes.

Whatever course you take, remember that change moves slowly in most cases. Even after witnessing shocking miracles, walking through the middle of the sea on dry ground, and being fed everyday with manna from heaven, the children of Israel had to wander around in the desert, moaning and groaning for forty years, until the stubborn old coots kicked the bucket and the new generation was willing to do what was required to inherit the Promised Land.

Though that happened thousands of years ago, the truth of it remains just as vibrant today. Stubborn old coots still come in many forms, and some of them aren't even old. Change generally requires that one or more persons must admit that maybe they had something wrong, and

that hurts pride. And pride is often one the biggest inhibitors to change, forward thinking, and forward acting.

This is especially true when that pride is in your own heart. Becoming a Seductioneer is a difficult transition for anyone with any pride (which is all of us), and though the world is full of Seductioneers who are advanced in age, generally the older a person is the more difficult it becomes for him to exercise the flexibility required. Life is forever blessed by flexibility. It is enabled through regular stretching of one's mind, opinions, and attitudes. It is enhanced by stretching beyond one's comfort zone, learning new things, and developing new skills. Never be afraid of the new. The only thing to fear is fear itself. And stagnation. And apathy. Which, if you count them all, is actually three things.

Oh, and maybe spiders too.

A demonstration of the fearless nature of the Sasquatch.

But I digress. Back to the question at hand.

Where do you get all your ideas?

I've heard this question regularly over the last two decades, and it seems to me that the frequency at which it is being asked is only increasing. I believe there's a reason for this—a correlation between a growing dearth of creativity and the ever-increasing bombardment of distractions in our already busy world. Our senses are constantly being inundated by a deluge of stimuli. And though some of this stimuli can inspire our creativity, much of it is rather two-dimensional, leaving us feeling like we've either been bingeing on junk food or are somewhere between waterlogged and drowned in the shallow end of the pool.

Some may believe this is simply a naturally harmless part of living in an ever-changing world. Conspiracy theorists, on the other hand, believe this is all part of a master plan of mind-numbing deceit put in place by the Illuminati and their cohorts to pacify us to the point where we will complacently fall in line, forget all creativity, and accept mediocrity in all its shades of beige. As a person who tries to avoid extremes, my opinion usually falls somewhere in the middle of these two schools of thought. But lately I've been reluctantly accepting that we may be sliding more toward the latter.

I recently interviewed a German engineer who lives in China and works in the automotive industry. When he graduated from college, he had grand ideas for innovation and creativity in his field. But over the past thirty-five years, he admitted that his aspirations and ideals have been squelched. "**Innovation**," he said, "**is dead**." He went on to explain that the automotive industry, as well as many other industries, is not looking for new ideas. Most industries, he insists, are looking for automation, simplification, and big profit. He explained that new ideas and innovation are expensive. They require retooling and rethinking. "Unless you have a half a million dollars," he admitted, "the most you're gonna get in terms of creativity or customization in my industry is a souped-up version of the floor model."

This engineer admitted that most of the new recruits they are hiring right out of school are doing as good of work after just six months on the job as he is doing. Why? Because the industry wants it to be that way. They're not looking for boat rockers. They're looking for people who can easily be replaced. They're looking for automatons who will merrily row their boats gently down the homogeneous stream. They're not concerned with passion or personality. They simply want to keep the investors happy by continually reporting record quarters. Colleges and universities are aware of what the labor force is looking for. Unlike in years past, this engineer suggested that universities are, in the best cases, subduers of and, in the worst cases, murderers of innovation and creative thought, conspiring with big business to produce skilled workers who are creatively indifferent. Universities often educate students on the same computers using the same software that the big companies use. This makes the transition from college to labor force more seamless but also speeds up the process of falling into what my friend Bert Compton refers to as a velvet-lined rut.

The velvet-lined rut is a real phenomenon in many careers and professions, as well as in every other endeavor in life. It's a trap that tends to feel less trap-like only because it's comfortable and cozy. We all have the potential of being lulled into submission by this rut. If the pay is adequate and the surroundings are agreeable, we usually don't protest. The things that bug us—that we'd like to change—are often forgotten or kicked down the road until the subtle yet constant friction, like a sharp piece of glass on the beach, wears down the edges until they become harmless and smooth. That may seem attractive to some, but if left in the rut, the whole piece of glass eventually disappears.

I've watched this happen in the lives of many of my friends—bright, creative people who entered the work force years ago with high ideals and aspirations but who slipped into the rut and slowly became complacent, lethargic, compliant, and submissive. It's easy to do. With opposition to change all around us, it's easy sometimes not to notice that we've been breathing this opposition in and have thereby been pacified

by its poison. If we lose the fight that's in us, it becomes ever easier to lose the entire war.

You may be asking yourself if the war for creativity and individuality is even a war worth fighting given all the challenges we face in the world today. My argument is that of all the wars to fight, this may be one of the most important. It is a war for the ownership and control of our very own hearts and minds.

Years ago, while in high school, I enrolled in what is still one of the most challenging courses I've ever taken. It was an AP U.S. History class taught by the brilliant and brutally honest George Henry. Mr. Henry is a gay black man who is active in both the ACLU and the NAACP. He taught like it was his job to challenge everything we knew or thought we knew. I loved his class and I hated it too. He made me think. He made me write. He made me cry. He made me stretch in very uncomfortable ways. But he made me open my mind to possibilities beyond what was obvious and apparent. Throughout the school year, three words remained scrawled across the top of his chalkboard: COMFORT RETARDS GROWTH.

This truth has never left me. I still think about it almost daily, twenty-seven years after the class ended. The velvet-lined rut may offer comfort, but it inhibits growth. And growth is one of the surest, most important indicators of life itself. Without growth, we're dead.

Benjamin Franklin said:

"Many people die at twenty-five and aren't buried until they are seventy-five."

The Sasquatches I know aren't necessarily afraid of death, but they tend to avoid being around it. Death is stinky and otherwise unattractive. I'm reminded of the Dr. Demento song with the truthful lyrics I used to hear when I was a kid: "Dead puppies aren't much fun." But heck, why stop at puppies? Dead people aren't much fun either. And if ol' Ben

Franklin had it right, we're probably surrounded by the breathing dead—folks who are comfortably and complacently waiting for their bodies to catch up with the rest of their lifeless existences. I for one have to believe there's a lot more to life than patiently waiting to keel over.

I grew up watching reruns of The Jetsons, the animated sci-fi sitcom set in the future. It got me excited for the future they presented, where every family had a compact spaceship of their own called an aerocar.

It's important to have science fiction, as the daydreams of its creators often become the reality of the future. In the case of the future presented by The Jetsons, I have to admit I'm really disappointed that I'm now in the future and the closest thing we have to an aerocar is an Astrovan, which, as you know, is really no comparison.

My point with bringing this up is that in early 60s when The Jetsons was created, America was in the Space Race with the Soviets. All sorts of creativity and innovation were at work, scientists moving as quickly as possible to create all forms of awesomeness. We had no limitations back then. Not even the sky was the limit anymore. And yet despite the rapid advances we saw during that period, somewhere, somehow, it slowly fizzled. Sure, we have a space station and satellites and cell phones, but the golden age of innovation and creativity we experienced during that time has slowed its pace at best and, at worst, is all but dead. The Cold War and the Space Race concluded, and people went back to comfortable living and riding around in basically the same cars that Henry Ford had designed and put into automation seventy years earlier.

Where are the dreamers we had back then? Why are we still driving on four wheels when the concept of the aerocar was given to us at least fifty years ago? How have we allowed ourselves to become so comfortable in the velvet-lined rut that our growth has been retarded? When are we going to allow the Kiss of the Sasquatch to once again jump-start our creativity?

A cheeky Sasquatch at Carhenge, Alliance, NE.

Wait, I thought you were going to tell us where you get your ideas.

I will, I promise. But a short history lesson might offer some context.

Over the last nearly two hundred years, our world has gone through a series of innovative fits and starts, proving that change can be both good and bad. The Industrial Revolution, for example, changed the lives of many through automation and mechanization. It made things inexpensive, allowing the common man to have more stuff, thereby creating and celebrating an appearance of wealth. People moved to the city to take "safe" jobs in the factories. They left the dirt and the farms for a better, richer life. And in the process, all sorts of chaos ensued.

Besides the big problems like sending children to work in factories, sweatshops, and slaughterhouses, people were no longer content with the two outfits they had to choose from. A walk in the woods or a buggy ride in the countryside gave way to chopping down the woods and paving the countryside. Steam-powered paddle boats and locomotives opened

the wilderness to advancement and expansion. The horseless carriage quickly evolved as Ford created a vehicle for the masses, "available in any color, as long as it is black." And though the Sasquatches of creativity sparked the imagination of many inventors during this era, industrialization also marked the early beginnings of the Sasquatch's decline.

Recognizing the negative direction and decline of quality brought on by industrialization, the Sasquatches inspired several anti-industrial counterrevolutions like the Arts and Crafts movement in Britain and America. These movements rebelled against the "more is more" mentality and focused instead on the creation of well-made durable goods that would last for generations. The movements rejected the inferior, soulless, and disposable products of industrialists in favor of the well-crafted items of skilled individual craftsmen.

The Arts and Crafts movement unfortunately met its doom with the advent of the Great Depression. Many are unaware of the fact that lean financial times also affect the morale of the Sasquatches, who both inspire and feed on the creative hopes and dreams that are so often dashed during recessions.

Industrialization also took a hit during this era. But with bigger infrastructure and better financial backing, the industrialists held onto their shorts while the craftsmen slowly and painfully lost theirs. With the declaration of war, the industrialists were far better suited to meet the needs of that war than the pacifist artists and craftsmen ever could have been. And by the time the war was over and the economy had recovered, many of the skilled craftsmen had aged out of the workforce, and the secrets of their trades with them.

The items that were created during the Arts and Crafts movement remain some of the most collectible pieces of craftsmanship ever. They were built to last, and last they have. I like to imagine the craftsmen who created them posthumously thumbing their noses at their industrialist rivals whose lives' work has long been forgotten.

At the time of writing this book, I see a new rebellion rising up. And

the Sasquatches of the world are collectively breathing a sigh of relief that their long neglect and slumber may be over and their services might once again be required and appreciated. I'm not sure if this new rebellion will ever rise to the level of the famed Arts and Crafts movement, but masses of people are beginning to grow tired of living in a disposable world. For the first time in a couple of generations, people are feeling like more is not necessarily more. Quality is once again challenging quantity. And if that quality has human fingerprints on it—all the better.

People are growing tired of stuff. We're waking up to the reality that the unbridled accumulation of stuff doesn't equate to happiness—that no one can wear sixty pairs of shoes or thirty jackets. We're looking at our storage units filled to the gills with crap we once thought would make us happy—stuff we haven't even looked at for years in many cases—and realizing that the magic we once believed was tied to this crap is just smoke and mirrors and is only weighing us down, costing us money to store, and causing unnecessary stress.

I foresee that in the coming years, people will divest themselves of this crap. Storage units will be emptied and shuttered. People will free themselves of the burdens of stuff. Experiences with friends and loved ones will take the place of empty, lifeless gifts. And there will come a renewal of interest in the old arts and crafts—things that were created by the human hand with the human experience in mind. People will rebel against the mass produced and seek after the one-of-a-kind items that are high in quality and originality.

In a world that seems to be ever unfolding in a cold, impersonal, unfeeling digital direction, people are and will increasingly be attracted to items that directly or indirectly allow them to connect with other humans. As an artist, I am witnessing this change of direction more and more each year.

Many people are surprised when they learn that I, a potter, purchase pottery mugs from potters I meet in my travels. Why? Because I love to sit down at a meal and reconnect with the potters I met at some point along my journey. I run my fingers over the marks their fingers left in

the wet clay, immortalized now in the fired stoneware. In many ways, these mugs are like the handwritten letters I've received over the years, which have been preserved and treasured while most of my digital correspondence has been either deleted or forgotten somewhere in my inbox. The humanity in each of us craves real connection with our fellow humans. And we can't find that in cold, lifeless, plastic—or in the digital realm.

As a potter, I've recognized for years that people can get a bowl or cup at Walmart for a fraction of the cost of its handmade distant cousin. And though the items from Walmart might serve the same objective, they are an impossible comparison for anyone looking for human connection. Knowing people will use my pottery for years to come, I do my best to imbue it with all the positivity and love I can muster. And people feel it. And they come back for more. I've learned that most folks want to share gifts that are unique and meaningful and that have life in them, and I'm grateful to be able to create work that fills that need.

A particularly photogenic Sasquatch at The Bean in Chicago, IL.

But wait, don't handmade items cost significantly more than stuff I can buy at Walmart?

The short answer is yes. You'll always pay more for an item that's been made by a human hand, regardless of where in the world it's made. But if you consider the fact that you're not just buying an interesting, unique item but that you're paying for some of the artist's time, blood, sweat, and tears, you can begin to understand both the value and the cost.

Handmade craftsmanship is sadly not something everyone can afford, and I certainly wouldn't want anyone to go into debt to outfit their home with handmade items. But I'd be willing to bet that if given the chance to choose between a human-made mug and a mass-produced one, most people would choose the handmade variety—either consciously or subconsciously.

I'm convinced that the chilliness of human interactions in our world today would warm significantly if we could learn to connect with each other—if we could recognize the humanity and goodness in each other. I'm reminded of the traditional Hindu greeting *Namaste*, which loosely means "I reverently salute you and acknowledge that we share a common piece of divinity. The best part of me honors the best part of you." How would all of our interactions with our fellow travelers be different if we could greet each person and recognize the common good in each other's souls? It seems unlikely that there would be a place for anger, hate, fear, malice, or prejudice.

It may seem like a great distance between connecting with a handmade mug and connecting with another human, but I'd like to suggest that the works of our hands and hearts can build bridges between us that commercial, industrial items never could. And I'd like to suggest that those connections can lead to connections with the Sasquatches in a neighborhood near you.

The truth is, all humans long for real, meaningful connections

and interactions, yet most of us are doing very little to seek out those connections. Between the thirty-five-plus hours a week that the average American spends in front of the TV and the nearly five hours a day he spends on his phone, we don't leave much time for making (real) friends. Many kids are not only losing their ability to have healthy, real, face-to-face conversations, they are also losing their ability to write sensible paragraphs without the use of emoticons or abbreviated words or phrases commonly used in text messaging. These tools may save time, but what is being lost in terms of culture, communication, and decency?

You may be thinking that I'm making a mountain out of a digital molehill or perhaps that I'm starting to sound like a geezer who needs to accept the inevitable reality that the world is changing. Both of these things may be true. But it saddens to me to watch virtual realities consistently and negatively changing actual realities. Time spent on social media is exploding while time spent in real social interaction is declining. In the process, the digitally enabled hookup culture is taking the place of the time-honored and certainly more meaningful practices of dating, courtship, love, and marriage. Is it any wonder that social anxieties and phobias are on the rise? It's like we all know there's an unsightly tumor growing on society's neck, but none of us are willing to either acknowledge it or do anything about it.

Yeah, why is that?

Because we've fallen into the blasted velvet-lined rut.

It's convenient and entertaining and loaded with immediate gratification, and we find all of that really sexy. But beyond just the sex appeal, digital interactions are so much easier and potentially less messy and engaging than real interactions. By avoiding the mess and time required of real interactions, we free up all sorts of time. But instead of using that time to be creative or engage in meaningful interactions with our friends and loved ones, we rejoice in the chance to spend even

more time with our digital distractions, sinking us further into creative stupefaction and social oblivion.

The Sasquatches have been watching this movement with abject horror. Since the beginning of time, they've been warned by generations of holy men who have shared their wilderness retreats that the time would come when men's hearts and creative fires would grow cold. They've known for years that the fulfillment of these prophecies would lead us into enslavement. By our own addictions to the works and creations of conspiring men who attempt to override our freewill, we are easily led down crooked paths where we forget who we are and the unlimited potential we have. The Sasquatches are also aware that the future is owned by those who create it. Endlessly optimistic, they continually reach out, trying to inspire anyone who's inclined to be open to creative ideas. They recognize they've been fighting a losing battle for many years, but they have hopes that books like this will inspire men and women, boys and girls to stop the madness; open their eyes, hearts, and minds to potential countermovements; and, in the process, help to save the world from creative poverty and devastation.

An observant Sasquatch recognizing that many have stepped way off the trail that leads to happiness

So wait a minute, I thought this was a course on creativity—not doomsday prophecies!

Patience, Grasshopper! Patience!

My suggestion that our addictions to screens are slowly killing off the best parts of what we honor in humanity is not hyperbole. These addictions have already proven to negatively effect creativity, one of humanity's most noble graces.

But there is still plenty of hope. Recognizing the dire need to unite their efforts in helping to save the world from creative suicide, a convention was recently convened in Lauterbrünnen, Switzerland. (It's neutral, close to Geneva, but infinitely more beautiful and more appropriate for a convention of Sasquatches.) The International Conference of United Sasquatches for Creativity, or I.C.U.S.F.C. as they call themselves, met to discuss options, strategies, and attack plans for jump-starting the creativity of humans around the world. It was the largest convention of its kind since 1302, when the council met in Florence to begin the groundwork for the Renaissance. And we all know how that turned out!

Sasquatch representatives from every major continent and isle of the seas came together to voice their concerns, share ideas, and offer opinions on the best ways to proceed. As guests of the Host Chancellor, Sir Füsse Grande, my colleague, Harry von Lederhösen, and I relished the enormously creative chatter and action plans put forward by the I.C.U.S.F.C. We know their efforts alone won't be enough to turn back the sweeping tide of apathy, mediocrity, and stagnation that has engulfed our world, but it's a positive start. We have hope that as more humans embrace the vision and excitement of this movement, together we'll be able to break the chains of indifference and elevate the vision and future of the world.

I already mentioned that this book is an invitation to join the revolution. It was while Harry and I were at this I.C.U.S.F.C gathering

that we received the commission for this book. We hope it will offer a solid foundation on which you and others like you who are anxious to make progress toward a new renaissance can build your platform.

There is much to be done and no time to lose. We can use all the help we can get. Our tasks are many and include, but are not limited to, inspiring others; eliminating mediocrity; and introducing the new ideas, philosophies, and practices outlined by the Lauterbrünnen Conference.

One of our first tasks is to find immediate housing for our friendly Sasquatches. Our furry friends have agreed to come out of the woods and hideaways until the crisis has passed. Thousands of host families are needed to offer food and shelter to these normally elusive Sasquatches. It will be a beautiful experience that you and your family will remember for the rest of your lives.

Have you considered inviting a Sasquatch into your home but aren't sure of the requirements? Don't worry. You're definitely not the first. The I.C.U.S.F.C. has asked me to discuss some of the most common questions asked by people contemplating the adoption of a Sasquatch.

Will they eat much?

No. Though the Sasquatches are generally a hungry lot, they tend to care for themselves and are surprisingly good cooks, capable of creating delicious, healthy meals with just a few basic ingredients. Don't be surprised if your whole family is soon eating foods they've never even tried before. Plus, with their creativity at work in your kitchen, it's likely that you'll discover the same phenomenon that many other early Sasquatch adopters have already reported: a food budget that stretches further than ever before.

Do they require their own bedrooms?

No. Sasquatches may be naturally shy and elusive, but not because of privacy issues. And because they don't sleep, there's no need for a bed. If you have an old recliner available for them, move it out into the yard. They will likely be interested in using it for stargazing and short rests.

Do they clean up after themselves?

Great question. Unfortunately, there's no quick answer to this one. It largely depends on the projects they may be involved in. We like to warn people that the creative Sasquatches can be quite messy, and the messes may stick around until a project is complete, at which time it's imperative that you require your Sasquatch to clean up his mess before starting a new project. They are generally compliant, but if you regularly entertain guests in your home, you may want to offer your Sasquatch a space that won't need to be straightened up more than once a month. The International Sasquatch Cleanup Day is the first Saturday of each month, at which time it's common for your Sasquatch to manically clean every nook and cranny in the house. Oh, and don't be surprised if he tries to enlist the help of all members of the family in his cleaning rituals.

Are they safe around children?

Absolutely! Don't let their shaggy hair, yellowed nails, or oversize feet fool you; Sasquatches are perfectly harmless. They will actually fill your children's heads with all sorts of creative ideas, helping them to

develop their imaginations. Don't be surprised if your normally boring kids are building forts and climbing trees by the end of the first week.

In pilot programs throughout the world, the young children of parents who adopt a Sasquatch get better grades, demand fewer hours of screen time, communicate in full sentences for the first time in their lives, develop their imaginations in innumerable ways, and gain exponentially more confidence than they ever had before. Many moms actually report wishing they could adopt a Sasquatch for each of their children. And though we would love to make that a reality at some point in the future, we want to make sure everyone who wants a Sasquatch has a chance to adopt one before we open things up for seconds.

Despite their hairy nature, Sasquatches love the beach.

What activities will our Sasquatch be expecting to do with our family?

Sasquatches are not picky, but they especially like to be invited to participate in any activity that requires movement and thought. You won't need to save a place for them on the sofa in front of the TV. (Sasquatches actually believe that TV sucks your soul out of your body through your nose, leaving you lethargic and brain-dead). But feel free to take them with you to church, the pool, the park, the library, the mountains—basically, any activity you enjoy, they will likely enjoy too. Of the families surveyed, 99% said they actually enjoyed all of their activities even more when a Sasquatch was with them. And many who said they had never before enjoyed hanging out with their families changed their tune completely when under the influence of the Sasquatches.

Do they shed?

Of course. They're covered from head to toe in long fur, for crying out loud! But ten out of ten adoptive families said they actually liked it. The Sasquatches hate waste and have found ingenious ways to make use of their shed fur. Your Sasquatch will arrive at your home knowing how to knit. Need a sweater to wear to that Christmas party? Just ask your Sasquatch. Socks and sweaters are standard products made by all Sasquatches, but they also take special requests including, but not limited to, hats, scarves, afghans, mittens, and even lingerie. "Your imagination is their only limitation". ™

How soon can I get my own Sasquatch?

Applications for Sasquatch adoptions are being accepted now! When we receive your application, we will immediately send out an

A.S.M. (Apathy and Stagnation Meter) to set up in your home for seven full days. This meter has been designed to help us assess the chi in your home and match you with a qualified Sasquatch. Then, after a routine house visit to make sure your home is properly outfitted with sufficient creative supplies, you will be able to select your Sasquatch from at least three individuals who will be identified from the larger pool of eligible Sasquatches using our carefully engineered matrix. After you and your family select the one you feel will best serve your needs, your Sasquatch should arrive within three (3) to ten (10) business days, depending upon the distance they must travel. Rest assured, we are partnering with our friends at UPS for expedited delivery to a neighborhood near you. "What can Brown (fur) do for you?"

How long will my Sasquatch stay?

Though it's likely that you'll want to make your Sasquatch a permanent member of your family, the Sasquatch Adoption Program (S.A.P.) has been designed for short-term adoptions only. You should not plan on keeping your Sasquatch any longer than six months. Some stay for much shorter times. In rare, extreme cases, Sasquatches may be adopted for up to a year. We anticipate that as more families become familiar with the S.A.P., we may have to shorten adoption times to keep up with the demand. It is important to keep in mind that the S.A.P. was designed to jump-start your family's own creativity and not to become a permanent crutch.

It may also be helpful to keep in mind that after your Sasquatch has moved on to another home and family, you can still arrange for it to visit your home for holidays, birthday parties, or other special occasions. And trips to your Sasquatch's homeland for regular tune-ups are strongly encouraged.

What does a Sasquatch jump start feel like?

To our knowledge, no two individuals have ever reported exactly the same experience. And though they vary wildly, some commonalities include feelings of euphoria, insatiable restlessness, vibrant aha moments, vivid dreams, and intense moments of unparalleled imagination. If your jump start is legitimate, your mind will be given jolts of creativity that may express themselves in a wide range of experiences. If you act on those jolts immediately, you'll recognize that more jolts will come, pushing you further and further toward fulfilling the measure of your creation. Those who are slow to respond to their jump starts have reported uncomfortable bouts of diarrhea, nausea, cold hands and feet, and chronic halitosis. Should you experience any of these symptoms, it is imperative for you to contact your Sasquatch Advisory Counselor (SAC) immediately, explain the symptoms and your reasons for delayed action, and ask for another jolt. He will likely tease you and call you a procrastinator in a variety of languages. But if you're persistent and say, "Pretty please with sugar on top," he will likely encourage your Sasquatch to respond positively. A little sugar goes a long way.

Could you use a creative jump start in your life? Does this sound like the perfect program for you and your family? We hope it does. The measures the I.C.U.S.F.C has taken to address this Astronomical Creativity Crisis (ACC) are completely unprecedented. Never before has the Society for Socially Responsible and Creative Sasquatches (S.S.R.C.S) even considered the possibility of their members being temporarily adopted by humans for the purpose of Creative Rehabilitation (CR).

Since time immemorial, those who have enjoyed interactions with the elusive and creative Sasquatches have had to work their buns off to locate, track, and seduce them. Because of this history, a certain cadre of the I.C.U.S.F.C feel like the program will make it too easy for humans to enjoy interactions with the Sasquatches. Due to this faction's very persuasive arguments, the I.C.U.S.F.C has unanimously voted to allow the S.A.P. to be available only for a limited time. So get your applications sent in today! The S.A.P. may end without warning, and humankind may be left in the creative dark.

Little known fact, Sasquatches love to picnic with strangers.

So, if I sign up for this program or decide I want to become a Seductioneer, what should I expect to gain?

As with nearly every other challenge in life, the answer to this question will depend entirely on:

- how far you're willing to go
- how hard you're willing to work
- how open minded you're willing to become
- how many of your fears you're willing to let go

As we ask you these questions, we recognize that the answer needs to be all yours—you can't look around and see what others are giving or doing and make your determinations according to peer pressure. We also recognize that these are not easy questions to answer. Each person's answer needs to be entirely personal. We have watched in shock and dismay as peer pressure has led many would-be Seductioneer candidates to embrace instead the far more common expressions of mediocrity, apathy, and stagnation. If you haven't noticed, these choices and the acceptance of this mentality have driven the world into what we call Creative Lethargy, or CL.

We've found in the last few decades that CL is wreaking havoc around the world. When it was first detected, we believed it would be only a short-lived fad—that it would be rejected quickly and that people would respond with a demand for a return to higher standards. But we have noticed that far too many people have embraced an It's-Good-Enough-Mentality. When people aren't willing to even go the first mile, it's hard to convince them that a second mile is a good idea. And this becomes even more difficult when people look around and see mediocrity everywhere. The world is in dire need of more people who embrace the ancient but often neglected virtue of excellence.

Our invitation to you is to just say NO to mediocrity. Stop the bankrupting of creative ideas, turn off the distractions, put on your work gloves, and fully embrace the Code of the Seducutioneer.

Code of the Seductioneer

On my honor, I will do my best to do my duty to pursue a creative life.

Where I find mediocrity, I will do all I can to replace it with excellence.

Where I find sluggishness, I will do all I can to replace it with diligence.

Where I find apathy, I will do all I can to replace it with enthusiasm.

Where I find creativity, I will do all I can to welcome and promote it.

Where I find color, innovation, and inspiration, I will do all I can to embrace it.

I will hear no mediocrity.

I will speak no mediocrity.

I will think no mediocrity.

But I will do all in my power to create excellence, foster excellence, and aspire to excellence.

In short, by adopting the Code of the Seductioneer as your own personal declaration, you commit to putting your head, heart, and hands into making this a brighter, creativer, and excellenter world. You are joining a worldwide league of people who share in your values as we promote and pursue excellence in huge variety of excellent ways.

So, who are these Seductioneers and what are they like?

We are artists, craftspeople, thinkers, poets, dreamers, doers, musicians, performers, professionals, and magic-bean buyers who have embraced the goals of excellence in all we do, think, and say. We are creative individuals who have chosen to buck tradition and strike out on the road less traveled.

You might guess that the traffic on this road is pretty minimal, and you'd be right. But we've found that the travelers we encounter are colorful, friendly, and interesting. In fact, there is nary a bore among us. It's a rather ragtag group of folks, but we always find each other to be some of the liveliest, most thoughtful, and most fun-loving weirdos you could ever imagine. Though we work in different media, we all seem to have one thing in common: We bear the mark of the Sasquatch!

What exactly does that mark look like?

We've often been asked to help identify and define the mark of the Sasquatch. This is a difficult thing to do, but for those of us who are aware of it, we recognize it in others and ourselves in the form of an insatiable itch.

The Itch is a common side effect of interacting with a Sasquatch. It has been described in numerous ways, but some of the more eloquent descriptions include:

"…a chronic itch, deep in my soul that makes it nearly impossible to sit still."

"…an itch that no amount of scratching can satisfy…the itch to explore, the itch to create, the itch to discover and dream and be."

"…an itch that only grows itchier with a scratching, often intensifying just by getting off the couch, or recognizing the swift and unstoppable passage of time, or the thoughts of far away places, or the smell of rain, or a memory of the sea…"

"…an itch whose only hope of satisfaction comes from being anxiously and perpetually engaged in creative endeavors."

"…an itch that is strongly exacerbated when one is exposed to the scent of stagnant waters and stale, comfortable places."

But another interesting commonality is that those who experience The Itch rarely consider this a malady. In fact, in a recent survey of Seductioneers conducted around the globe, everyone who responded said The Itch was something they looked forward to, knowing new ideas would come as they worked at scratching The Itch.

If you have experienced symptoms like this in your own life, it is likely that you may have unknowingly been exposed in some way to the Kiss of the Sasquatch. This is a good thing. The kiss has the ability to open the doors to creative development and discovery. So go ahead and scratch The Itch, but know that the most effective way of doing so, as one of the responders to our survey suggested, is in "…being anxiously and perpetually engaged in creative endeavors."

Sasquatches: there ain't no mountain they can't climb.

So, back to the question that started all of this:

"Where do you get all your ideas?"

Over the years, I've often given in to the temptation to answer this question with creative answers like, "I buy them by the dozen from the bewitched elves of the Land of Fantastico" or "I sold my soul to the devil's sassy sister-in-law in exchange for a lifetime of fresh ideas."

But in reality, I'm not even sure if the devil has a sister-in-law, and I've heard those pesky elves are far more trouble than they're worth, eating all your food and leaving you to clean up the mess.

But I do believe this question deserves an answer, and not just any old answer will do. As I've thought about this question over the years, I've recognized that it's a question that cannot be satisfactorily answered with a sentence or two, no matter how well thought out and well delivered. It's a big question with an even bigger answer—an answer that can change the way you think and live and act. It's an answer that's way bigger than me and you and everyone else who ever asked the question

and went searching for answers. In fact, it's an answer that can change the whole stinkin' world and maybe even the entire universe.

There are probably lots of folks who could write this book. And there are certainly other books out there about creativity. I have a small stack of them that I've acquired over the years as I've wondered how other creative folks have answered this most oft-repeated question.

If you picked up this book, it's likely that you've got a creative itch that needs some scratching. My goal in writing this book is not to offer you the magical, miraculous scratch that will satisfy your lifelong afflictions with The Itch. Rather, my goal is to remind you that ignoring The Itch—hoping it will just go away—has brought you little to no real relief. Let's face it: The Itch needs scratching. It will never leave you alone. You may have tried your best to eliminate it by starving it, ignoring it, or medicating it. If you're honest, you've also attempted to suppress it with hours of talk therapy in which you have tried to justify your neglect of it by telling yourself you're trying to be practical, pragmatic, and sensible.

Uhh, yeah, as a matter of fact, I have told myself that.

But it hasn't worked, has it?

No, as a matter of fact, not at all.

You wanna know why?

Yes, please!

It's because your idea of what's practical, pragmatic, and sensible is probably nothing more than a bunch of bunk. Nonsense. Absurdity. Foolishness. Stuff your parents or teachers told you that you've been repeating for years without really stopping to think about it.

Keep it up, and The Itch will persist forever, waking you up at night, leaving you tossing and turning.

So what am I supposed to do?

Well, to begin with, I'd like to suggest that there's for a reason for that insatiable itch. It's an integral part of who you are. And you won't ever be able to get rid of it any more than you could comfortably rid yourself of that incessant beating inside your rib cage. Like the body you received at birth, your creativity is an indivisible part of you. It was there from the beginning, before you could talk or walk or feed yourself. If you were lucky, you had big people around you who nurtured that creative you with music, stories, dancing, color, and hands-on art projects. If you weren't so lucky, your itch may be deeply suppressed, but it's still there, bubbling to the surface from time to time, surprising you with its compelling push or pull to go, to be, to do.

As a Christian, I grew up with the belief that I am a child of God. And if I am, that means you certainly are too, whether you know it yet or not. And as the offspring of God—the Creator of the universe—we have been endowed with some of His magic. He has given us talents and freewill, enabling us to use and develop those talents for both good and evil or to neglect and forget them altogether. The choice is ours. And we make that choice every day of our lives.

The two most important days in your life
are the day you are born
and the day you find out why.
—Mark Twain

There are many levels of wisdom in Mr. Twain's words. Birth and life itself are probably best valued when we recognize them for the gifts they are. But gifts have little value until they're unwrapped, assembled, and fully appreciated. We all know folks who seem to understand this better than most, whose lives are full and bright and beautiful. Perhaps we have a little bit of life envy toward people like that. That's understandable. After all, we all want a life that is full, bright, and beautiful, right?

Yeah. So, what do they have that I don't?

I've wondered this myself many times over the course of my life as I've encountered people who seem to be living a brighter life than I am. I've found that many such people are generous and open and willing to share their wisdom and experience with those who are sincere and willing to put in the work.

That last bit is important. Work. It may seem as if it is easier for some people to achieve happiness, wealth, and esteem than it is for you. But I don't believe it's beyond any of us to achieve a high level of all of the above if we're willing to work for it.

In 1854, Henry David Thoreau published his book, *Walden*, which documents the two years, two months, and two days he spent in a tiny cabin on the shores of Walden Pond just outside of Concord, Massachusetts. As he says,

"I went to the woods because I wished to live deliberately, to front only the essential facts of life, and see if I could not learn what it had to teach, and not, when I came to die, discover that I had not lived."

Over the course of his time at Walden Pond, Thoreau made many profound discoveries about both himself and the nature of humankind in general. Thoreau's desire to truly live prompted him to write many

volumes, promoting, among other ideas, the need for an open mind and a willingness to push against the limits imposed upon us by our society. One of my favorites is:

"The mass of men lead lives of quiet desperation, and go to the grave with the song still in them."

The truth Thoreau penned one 164 years ago is just as true today as it was then. Be it through fear, selfishness, laziness, procrastination, or apathy, the bright songs of men and women continue to be muted, if not lost entirely. And the world is only darker for it.

But I submit that it doesn't have to be this way. I submit that the unique songs we each have to sing are necessary to illuminate the world around us. And we can't just hum a few bars half-heartedly. I'd like to suggest that in order for it to really count, we need to climb up high and sing our song with all the ferocity of what Walt Whitman referred to as a "barbaric yawp!"

"I sound my barbaric yawp over the roofs of the world."—Walt Whitman

The Sasquatch never fears the exclamation of his own yawp.

So wait, why is yawping so important?

Because the truth is that we cannot be truly happy unless we do.

There is no joy in mediocrity. There is no joy in being half-hearted. There is no joy in apathy, procrastination, indifference, neglect, selfishness, or laziness. I have lived long enough and observed enough people to know that those vices yield only regret, discontent, unhappiness, and contempt for oneself and others. They create misery. They have no other choice. There's nothing in them that's capable of creating anything but misery. And no matter how you spin it, there can never be even a drop of long-term fun to be found in misery. To think otherwise is to plant rocks and hope they'll grow into flowers.

So, what's this song that's inside of you? What are you doing with it? Are you singing it over the rooftops of the world, or are you letting something keep you from it?

There is only one you. And those God-given talents you arrived with have either been growing and developing over the years or they've been starved and neglected. There's not a lot of middle ground here. But our past is history—a history that doesn't have to define our future. How great would it be if we woke up tomorrow (and every day after that), looked at ourselves in the mirror, and repeated to ourselves the last lines of William Earnest Henley's poem "Invictus":

I am the master of my fate:
I am the captain of my soul.

I fear that far too many of us have bought into the idea that we are far less than the masters of our fates and the captains of our souls. Fear is often the culprit. Maybe we've been held back by fear of failure, fear of limitations, fear of being mocked. But a life constrained by fear is really no life at all. Indeed, everything you want in life is on the other side of fear.

So, when are you going to start living? When are you going to free yourself of the fears that have held you back? When are you going to remember that you are a child of God—the Master and Creator of the universe.

For God hath not given us the spirit of fear;
but of power, and of love, and of a sound mind.
—2 Timothy 1:7

How would your life be different moving forward if you made every decision based on love rather than fear? It's an intriguing idea, isn't it?

But could it work? Can you really do this?

Are you willing to try?

But, wait…I thought you were going to tell us where you get all your ideas! This seems like it's going off on a very different tangent again!

It totally wouldn't surprise me. I've heard Ben has ADD.

Ha ha! I have no doubt about that, but I'm not sure it is a tangent. I mean…if fear is the opposite of love and fear holds us back from being creative, could love and creativity be cousins?

Hmmmm. Interesting idea. I guess I've never thought about that.

Well, I'd like to submit to you that they are indeed cousins, tied together by the same Creator who ties us together as members of the human family.

But wait…if love and creativity are cousins, wouldn't they share some family resemblances? You know, like big noses and receding hairlines?

Well, yeah, they would. And if you'll take a look, you'll find that love and creativity do share many of the same attributes and ideals. And they work together. Love is creative. You can't express it without creating good feelings. And creativity—at its best—is full of love, right?"

Hmmm. I see what you mean…………But wait, if that's true, do you think that love might be the answer? Do you think that love is the secret to discovering creative ideas and solutions?

Now we're finally talking! Love is always the answer—to everything—and has been from the very beginning.

The very beginning, huh? This sounds vaguely familiar… Oh, my gosh, I just remembered the first words of the Bible…In the beginning, God created …

Very good! But have you ever stopped to wonder why He went to all the trouble?

Uhhh, no. I guess I haven't. Why do you think he did it?

Think about it.

Uh, well, maybe he was bored, or…… Wait a second…do you really think love is the answer…to EVERYTHING?

Absolutely! Love is unconditionally the purest, most powerful motivation.

God creates because He loves. And the love He plants in our hearts motivates us to do the same—for the same reasons. Creation—the art of putting our creativity to work—must be motivated by love and carry with it a portion of love if it is to have any ability to uplift, empower, and inspire others.

These ideas are pretty simple when it comes right down to it, but they're sometimes difficult to share in quick, easy sound bites that are short enough to fit within the 8.25 seconds of a modern American adult's attention span.

The difficulty only increases when I'm asked about the source of my ideas by a dude at an arts festival who has two beers in his hands; has at least two more in his belly; and is having difficulty standing up, let alone conversing or listening in a meaningful way. That dude usually gets a story about the inspirational choir of leprechauns under my bed that sings me sweet lullabies every night.

Why would you tell him that?

Because it's cute and quick and he won't remember what I said in ten minutes anyway. He doesn't *really* want to know.

What makes you so sure?

Three things: Sincerity. Humility. Patience.

I'm sure many other virtues are helpful in finding answers to life's big questions, but these three are essential. Without them, we shouldn't be surprised to get unhelpful answers to our half-hearted questions.

Creative ideas are out there—always—everywhere—and available to everyone. But many of us miss them, believe there's nothing new under the sun, or impatiently return to the status quo when the answers we seek don't come right away. Some of us ask for ideas without doing our homework, filling our card catalogs, or sacrificing anything. In my experience, neither God nor the universe ever works that way. Work has always been an eternal principle. Without it, nothing gets done. Without doing our due diligence in preparation for inspiration, we will limit our ability to receive. Without filling our card catalogs (see tip number 81 on the flip side) or filling them only with the common, mundane, and boring, we shouldn't expect clever bits of awesomeness to appear out of nowhere.

For millennia, scholars, clergy, and philosophers have argued over many aspects of the origin and/or creation of the world. The concept of ex nihilo, Latin for "out of nothing," has been tossed around like a hot potato.

So, is it possible to create something out of nothing?

For God, that's debatable. For us, it's impossible.

I've never been able to bake a batch of cookies without any ingredients. And even if I were missing only an egg or a stick of butter or a cup of sugar or flour, I would never expect things to turn out right if I went ahead without a key ingredient. It seems like it would be foolish to think otherwise.

These same concepts apply to all forms of creativity. As a potter, I've gained a lot of knowledge about my craft. I know about chemistry as it relates to glaze formulation, I understand some of the physics of fire, and I know how to form a bowl on the wheel. And though there's probably some crossover knowledge that I might share with a NASA engineer, I would be foolish to believe I could step into his shoes tomorrow and be ready to face his challenges. At the same time, that engineer, even if he

understood the physics of fire, would probably feel pretty helpless firing my kiln, calculating my glazes, or creating anything better than mud pies on my wheel.

When it comes to creativity, mastering the elements of your craft takes time, practice, knowledge, and patience. It requires learning the rules before learning which ones can be and must be broken in order to proceed creatively. Learning to use a recipe is a helpful way to start learning how to cook. But you don't become a creative, world-class chef without stepping away from the safety of the recipe at some point and striking out on your own. Additionally, somewhere along the line every good chef has to learn how to love—love his craft—love his ingredients—love his staff—love the people he serves. Without that love, any success he finds will be short lived. You've got to fuel the fire, and simultaneously you've got to love it.

Believe it or not, you are undoubtedly far more capable than you think you are. You have the potential to dream and create and become all that you can imagine, and much more. You have within you the possibility of thinking up things that have never existed. You have the ability to come up with solutions to some of the world's most pressing problems. You have it in you to create, to love, to become something uniquely awesome! So, what's the holdup?

Why are you stuck in a pattern of addiction, indecision, and indifference? Why are you letting life pass you by, marking its passing only by the timing of your favorite sitcoms? Deep inside you, you know there's more to life than what you've seen so far.

I've discovered recently that most creative blocks—perhaps most blocks in general—are not due to a lack of creativity but rather to a lack of confidence. We worry that we're not good enough; that we don't know enough; that we're not beautiful, smart, talented, or fast enough to follow our dreams. We worry that our muse has left our shores for an indefinite vacation and is incommunicado. We worry that without her, we are nothing.

But the truth is that your confidence is a big fat liar sometimes. You are enough of nearly all of the things that matter most. And the things you still lack can be gained with time and persistence. As it turns out, your muse isn't on vacation after all. Your confidence, deficit posing as a fire-breathing dragon, has kidnapped her and locked her away in the high turret of his castle. And, truth be told, she's getting really tired of waiting around for you to free her from the seven-headed monster you've created—that same beast you've been nourishing with your fears and apathy.

Your problem, it seems, is very common. That shouldn't make you feel any better. In fact, it should make you crazy. After all, you took the bait—hook, line, and sinker. Instead of doing the work to track down your muse and temper the dragon of low confidence with the sword of love, you've fallen into the tar pits of apathy. You can blame it on your friends if it makes you feel any better; after all, they're likely sitting next to you, blowing bubbles in that tar as they fart around, pretending to enjoy themselves.

This whole scenario reminds me of a quote by the Beach Boy Brian Wilson, who said:

"Beware the lollipop of mediocrity;
lick it once and you'll suck forever."

It's a funny quote with a powerful warning, but it's not entirely true. Yes, embracing the easy road of mediocrity does cause a person to suck, but it needn't be forever. We can learn from our mistakes. We

can conquer our confidence issues. We can pull ourselves out of those clingy tar pits of apathy. We can tell the fear that's been holding us back to take a hike. We can learn to love ourselves, our work, and our fellow travelers.

Okay, okay, but isn't all of that easier said than done

Sure. I'd be lying if I said any of those things were easy.

Yes, it's going to be one of the hardest but absolutely best things you'll ever do. It's gonna take time—a whole lotta time. It's gonna take work—a whole lotta work. But getting out of the velvet-lined rut, pulling yourself out of the tar pits of apathy—that's your only hope of changing the world. It's your only hope of making a difference for good. If you can learn to love and then stitch some love into everything you do, you'll have more friends and admirers than you'll know what to do with. If you can keep that admiration from going to your head, using it instead to fuel your confidence in your next creative project—and the one after that and the one after that—your life will only grow in meaning and understanding. There will be no limits to what you can do. If your desires are pure and selfless, if your reasons are filled with love for mankind, then God and his angels, the entire race of Sasquatches, and indeed all the universe will conspire to help you.

Seductioneers, the entire I.C.U.S.F.C. as well as my colleague Harry von Lederhösen and I wish you all the best as you move forward with your creative endeavors.

By combining the theory of Sasquatch seduction from this side of the book with the 101 helpful practice exercises on the flip side, you'll find that your creativity will be jump-started in no time.

Cheers to your journey, fellow Seductioneers!

More helpful hints about embracing the creative life can be found in Harry and Ben's forthcoming book, *How to Yodel with the Yeti.*

"Here's to the crazy ones. The misfits. The rebels. The troublemakers. The round pegs in the square holes. The ones who see things differently. They're not fond of rules. And they have no respect for the status quo. You can quote them, disagree with them, glorify or vilify them. About the only thing you can't do is ignore them. Because they change things. They push the human race forward. And while some may see them as the crazy ones, we see genius. Because the people who are crazy enough to think they can change the world, are the ones who do."

—Rob Siltanen (sometimes attributed to Steve Jobs, but he was quoting Rob.)

A survey was conducted during the International Conference of United Sasquatches For Creativity, or I.C.U.S.F.C. in Lauterbrünnen, Switzerland to help us understand where Sasquatches like to hang out. These are the top results of that survey. We would like to suggest that hanging out at such places and participating in such activities will likely influence the success of your Sasquatch seduction expeditions in very positive ways. Though this list is by no means comprehensive, it's a great place to start. Additional suggestions will be available in Ben's and Harry's forthcoming book, *How to Yodel With a Yeti*.

Places

- **Libraries and/or bookstores.** Some Sasquatches even suggest that hanging out in the kid's section and looking at children's books is a great place to revive dormant creativity. *(If you look at all like a kidnapper, be sure to take your own kid or grandkid with you to the kid's section so other parents don't think you're a creeper and call the cops.)* Give yourself the gift of a full day at the library to research anything you want. Take your sketchbook. Jump down every rabbit hole you encounter. Explore. Discover. Imagine. Do it again soon.
- **Museums.** Art, Natural History, Unnatural History, etc., Museums are a great source of inspiration. They are often quiet and offer a place of reflection and beauty.
- **Nature.** Mountains, rivers, sea, grasslands, your backyard, etc. Leave your phone at home or in your pocket. Take your sketchbook/journal and open yourself to Mother Nature. Walk, bike, climb, swim, skip, sit and simply experience all the magic that surrounds you.
- **The Hardware Store.** Spend a little time in the nuts and bolts

section. Peruse the paints. Sniff the lumber. You'll likely be amazed as how many Sasquatches you'll discover there.

- **Quiet places.** Yep, Sasquatches are known to hang out in quiet, peaceful places. Find your happy place. Go there often.
- **Arts festivals.** Most cities of any size have them. Go check them out. Spend some time talking to the artists and admiring their work. Take some art home with you. Sasquatches are attracted to homes where original artwork hangs on the walls. Surround yourself with beauty and you'll be surprised by the beauty that comes out of you.

Activities

- **Take a walk.** Fresh air does amazing things to promote creative thought.
- **Make a new friend out of a stranger.** While you're on your walkabout, stop and talk to people you meet along the way. Chances are they're looking for a Sasquatch too.
- **Start a new collection.** Acorns, bottle caps, rocks, snail shells, etc. Share your collection with others.
- **Lay on the grass and watch the clouds move across the sky.** It's probably been a few years since you've done this, but it's a great way to spend an afternoon, and a highly effective way to seduce a Sasquatch.
- **Crash the funeral or wedding of a stranger.** If anyone asks, make up a good story.
- **Get lost.** Drive or walk down streets you've never seen before. Drive into the countryside with no particular destination in mind. See where you end up. The Sasquatches will find you there.
- **Limit yourself to bicycle transportation for one week.** Like

many of these suggestions, getting out of old habits and opening your head to new ideas and experiences will enable the seeds of creative ideas to find fertile soil in that space between your ears.

- **Listen to new music and/or podcasts.** Ask friends for suggestions. There's some really great stuff out there that will broaden your mind and expand your ideas.
- **Take a cooking class.** Tired of variations on mac-n-cheese? Learn a new skill. Invest in your culinary future.
- **Make up a new game.** Start with a ball or balls of your choice. Add implements as they make sense—or don't. Make up goals, objectives, and rules. (Works best if children are involved and media is not.)
- **Turn off your phone for three whole days.** You'll likely sweat, squirm, itch, shake, and finally relax, clear your head, and see new things.
- **Dream up ten new names for your lover.** Sugar Muffin o' Love, Pumpkin Guts, Fire of My Loins, etc. If they're any good, you will breathe new life into your relationship. If they're bad… well, then at least you'll have something to laugh at.
- **Write a letter to a friend using real paper and ink.** Or, if you don't have much to say, send a postcard, writing your note on the back of postcard you create. (Cereal and cracker boxes are great sources for appropriate cardstock.) But don't limit yourself. The post office accepts a broad array of items. I once sent my girlfriend a "post coconut", writing my message on the brown husk and affixing a stamp. It arrived safely. She still has it. She is now my wife.
- **Clean out the storage unit, shed, or garage.** Throw out everything you haven't used in five years. If you haven't used it in five years, it's unlikely you ever will. No sense in paying rent or taking up space with something that no longer brings you joy. "Sentimentality is very expensive and often overrated," says the man with a "post coconut" in a box in his basement.

- **Rearrange your furniture.** Invite your kids, partner or friends to give their input, or better yet, lend a hand. You may end up moving it back the next day, but shaking things up is a great way to jumpstart your thinker.
- **Climb up on your roof and have a picnic with someone who would appreciate it.** (Don't do this if you are unstable on your feet, or if snow and/or ice are present.)
- **Write a free verse poem or haiku about your breakfast.**
- **Wear funny socks.** You may be the only one who ever knows, but you'll be surprised how liberating it feels to simply step away from the boring, mundane, and common. And crazy socks are a great way to start doing just that.
- **Drink more ginger ale.** 10 out of 10 Sasquatches say ginger ale's bite and effervescence is a great elixir for exciting dormant enthusiasm.
- **Create a new cookie.** You may need to look at a few recipes to make sure you're not going totally off the rails, but then set them aside and make one up. Put in your favorite things. Try something totally different—shredded carrots, peanut butter, wasabi peas, cream cheese, sunflower seeds, Skittles, etc. Take notes about what works and what doesn't. Share the bombs with your kids and the good ones with your neighbors.
- **Decide to become an inspiration rather than a warning to others.** That decision alone will push you a long way, and it's incredibly seductive to the Sasquatch.
- **Trust people.** Sure, a few will disappoint you, but trusting the world goes a long way to making it a kinder place. It's not as bad as you might think. Plus, extending trust lays the foundation for great friendships and meaningful relationships.
- **Travel as often as possible—even if it's only an hour away.** Getting out of your own headspace and seeing new territory is a great way to open your head and heart to the call of the Sasquatch.